HANDBOOK OF THE FRESHWATER FISHES OF INDIA

HANDBOOK OF THE FRESHWATER FISHES OF INDIA

GIVING THE CHARACTERISTIC PECULIARITIES OF ALL THE SPECIES AT PRESENT KNOWN, AND INTENDED AS A GUIDE TO STUDENTS AND DISTRICT OFFICERS.

CAPTAIN R. BEAVAN, F.R.G.S.

GYAN

Published by

Gyan Publishing House
5, Ansari Road
Daryaganj, New Delhi-110002
Phone: 011-47034999, 9811692060
E-mail: books@gyanbooks.com

Distribution Network
gyanbooks.com
India, USA, Canada, UK, Australia, France

ISBN: 978-81-212-8884-2 (PB)
First Published, 1877

2nd Impression 2023

Printed at: Gyan Press, Delhi.

HANDBOOK OF THE FRESHWATER FISHES OF INDIA
AUTHOR: CAPTAIN R. BEAVAN

HANDBOOK OF THE FRESHWATER FISHES OF INDIA.

HANDBOOK OF THE

FRESHWATER FISHES OF INDIA.

GIVING THE CHARACTERISTIC PECULIARITIES OF ALL THE SPECIES AT PRESENT KNOWN, AND INTENDED AS A GUIDE TO STUDENTS AND DISTRICT OFFICERS.

BY CAPTAIN R. BEAVAN, F.R.G.S.,

OF THE BENGAL STAFF CORPS,
CORRESPONDING MEMBER OF THE ZOOLOGICAL SOCIETY OF LONDON,
ASSISTANT-SUPT. IN THE SURVEY DEPARTMENT OF INDIA.

"The earth is full of the goodness of the Lord."

LONDON:
L. REEVE & CO., 5, HENRIETTA ST., COVENT GARDEN.
1877.

PREFACE.

IN preparing this work, I have tried to make it, as nearly as I could, what it professes to be, viz. a Hand-book. In fact, when commencing on it, I intended it as much for my own use as for that of others, to save perpetual references to and comparisons among various books and publications. When I first took up the study of Ichthyology I found, and still find, that the great difficulty is to know where to look for any particular information one requires: and I have therefore attempted to bring together, in a compact form, such items as I have found practically to be most frequently wanted. It may be some time before a complete work on the Indian Fishes, with full descriptions of their peculiarities and habits, and copiously illustrated, can appear; in the meantime I trust that this little work may supply a want, and perhaps assist in creating an interest in a subject that has at present but few students. My hope therefore is that this compilation (for it does not profess to be anything more than a compilation) may prove useful to my fellow-workers in this branch of zoology, as a book of reference; and that those who have not time or inclination to study the subject, may find herein a ready means of discovering the names of any fishes they may come across, and wish to identify.

To the late Dr. Jerdon I am indebted for first directing my attention to this interesting study, and for much help in mastering the primary difficulties.

From Dr. Günther, of the British Museum, I have received much kind assistance, notably in the revision of my List of Species.

I have made free use of such works and publications on the subject as I have been able to procure. Among others, Surgeon Major Day's Monograph of Indian Cyprinidæ, published in the Journal of the Asiatic Society of Bengal; his Report on the Indian Fisheries, and various papers in the Proceedings of the Zoological Society of London; also the works of Dr. Francis Hamilton (formerly Buchanan) and Dr. John M'Clelland.

I have been under the disadvantage of being far from the reach of any standard library or large museum to refer to in cases of difficulty. This drawback would have been indeed fatal, were it not for the British Museum Catalogue, in which all the information previously published by various authors has been laboriously collected together. Such species as are insufficiently known, or which for any reason are doubtful, I have placed apart in an Appendix.

I have collected all the Synonyms by which the various species have been from time to time described by different authors, together with such vernacular Indian names as I have been able to extract from various writers, or have myself become acquainted with, into an Index. By this means I have avoided the necessity of loading the descriptions of species with a crowd of names.

The illustrations have been taken from fresh, or living, specimens. I should have liked to have introduced many more plates, only that it would have added very considerably to the cost of publication.

I have the satisfaction of seeing, in the papers of the last English Mail, that the subject of the Geographical Distribution of Species, alluded to in Chapter III., has attracted attention at the recent meeting of the British Association. As remarked in Chapter I. the strictly fresh-water fishes afford a valuable guide towards the elucidation of many interesting problems connected with this subject.

It was not till after the manuscript of this Handbook had been sent to London for publication, that I became aware that Dr. Day was bringing out a very elaborate work on Indian Marine and Freshwater fishes.

Had I known this sooner, I would have avoided the possible imputation of wishing to put myself in competition with this indefatigable naturalist, and would have left the work alone. Even now I would retire from the field if I thought my publication could injuriously affect the success of his work. It will rather, I believe, have a contrary effect. The two books are essentially different in plan, size, and price, and the one may, I venture to hope, rather assist the other by stimulating an interest in the subject among some who have not hitherto had their attention directed this way.

It would certainly have been more satisfactory to me if I had had the advantage of seeing Dr. Day's new work before compiling my own book. He has doubtless collected a considerable amount of information not hitherto published, and has probably described some new species.

It must be remembered, however, that no work on Natural History can be considered complete in the sense of containing all possible information; what I have given here is fully sufficient, I trust, to fulfil the object of the book, and will be found, I hope, fairly accurate so far as it goes.

CONTENTS.

ILLUSTRATIONS.

ERRATA.

Page 29, last line but one, *for* "Anabas scandeus" *read* "Anabas scandens."

Page 98, line 20, *for* "Lounsius" *read* "Leuciscus."

Page 129, first line, *for* Callichdous" *read* "Callichrous."

Page 166, line 5, *for* "lata" *read* "lala."

Page 181, line 6, also line 10 and line 15, *for* "Eutroplus" *read* "Etroplus."

HANDBOOK OF INDIAN FRESH-WATER FISHES.

CHAPTER I.

ON ICHTHYOLOGY IN GENERAL, AND THAT OF THE INDIAN FRESH WATERS IN PARTICULAR.

ICHTHYOLOGY, or the Study of Fishes, is one of the least popular branches of Natural History; the reason being probably that the element in which fishes live, prevents their peculiarities and habits being brought so prominently before our every-day notice as are those of creatures living on dry land.

Many people are led by the beauty of flowers to direct their attention to the study of botany, or by the cheerful songs and bright plumage of birds to investigate their natural history. Many a time has the acquisitiveness of childhood, directed at first to the collection of butterflies, or birds' eggs, ripened into the scientific inquisitiveness of later years, and made itself manifest in due course of time through the patient labour of an ornithologist or an entomologist.

But fishes do not force themselves upon our attention in this manner, they do not show to advantage when taken out of the water, indeed to a superficial observer there seems little difference between one kind of fish and another; in fact, most people would recognise them more readily when on the dinner table, clothed only in their appropriate sauce, than when seen in their natural state with all their wonderful arrangements of fins and scales, and other adjuncts complete.

It is only of late years that any attempt has been made, by the establishment of large public aquariums, to enable people in general to form any idea of the domestic life of fish at home.

And yet, when one comes to know a little about fish, it becomes manifest that they yield in interest to no other class of created things,—whether we consider their wonderful variety, or the beauty of some species, and the strange shapes and hideous appearance of others, or the peculiarities of their habits.

The study of Ichthyology has certainly peculiar difficulties, but it has also advantages of its own.

One thing which, in the eyes of many people, would detract from its interest, is the fact that it is hardly possible to establish a "collection" of fishes.

A great many people consider natural history to be an affair of cabinets, and drawers, and portfolios, and the more odds and ends of sorts they can collect together the more they are pleased. (This, as I before remarked, is the childish, not the practical view of the subject.) Now, fish don't lend themselves to this kind of thing; if you want to see them to advantage you must study them while they are fresh, or if possible alive, or, best of all, in their natural element.

You can certainly preserve specimens in bottles of spirits, but they do not retain their beauty in this way, and except in a public museum for reference and comparison, such specimens have no interest. Thus the ichthyologist has no trophies to gloat over; "nothing to show" for all his trouble and investigations.

Another thing that may at the outset serve to deter people from studying the natural history of fishes, is the formidable appearance of the nomenclature, and the amount of scientific and anatomical terms that abound in all books on this subject.

Few attempts have as yet been made to popularise the subject, and as yet, it may be said, the subject is comparatively a new one; the great object hitherto has been to collect facts, to find out new species, to compare them one with another, and to collect them into natural groups according to their affinities; in short, to classify them.

For this kind of work the utmost accuracy is necessary; a rough description of a fish, such as would convey some idea of what it was like to a person who had not studied the subject, would be perfectly useless for purposes of classification, as it would probably omit the very points which it would be necessary to know in order to assign to the fish its proper position in the system.

Each family, and each genus, has certain distinctive peculiarities which are common to all the fishes in that family or genus, and at the same time there are certain other points which are inclined to be variable in that family, or that genus, and by the aid of such peculiarities is one species to be discriminated from another.

For example, the Browns might be characterised by a hooked nose, and the Joneses by a cast in the eye, but to describe the difference between two Joneses, say Tom and Harry, you would have to notice some other detail that was variable in the Jones family.

To give a familiar expression to my argument. Suppose a traveller saw a monkey for the first time, and described it as "a creature with a long tail, that lives in trees." Obviously such a description as this would throw no light on its classification, as it might equally refer to a squirrel, or to a lizard. On the other hand, if he was to describe it as a "quadrumanous mammal," a naturalist would know at once what kind of a creature it was, even though monkeys had never previously been heard of.

For this reason it has been necessary, in describing new species of fish, to use the most strictly technical terms, of the exact meaning of which there can be no doubt, and to avoid ordinary colloquial expressions, which might bear various meanings.

The names again which have been bestowed on fishes and on the groups into which they are collected, being generally derived from the Greek, have a formidable aspect. This difficulty, however, soon wears off; and when the meaning of the terms become known, they afford in many cases a valuable aid in remembering the chief characteristic of the group or species.

Who, I would ask, finds any difficulty in remembering such terms as "Fuchsia," "Geranium," or "Hippopotamus," which they are accustomed to? Few harder words than these are to be met with in Ichthyology.

(N.B. A useful little word to be familiar with is the Greek "Ichthys," a fish, which forms part of many names, and has rather an uncompromising look about it.)

Now, however, that the foundation, so to speak, has been firmly laid, there is no longer the necessity, in discussing the fishes of a well explored region, for instance, the fresh-water fishes of the Indian peninsular, of overloading our descriptions with a mass of technical terms. We need no longer work from the particular to the general, and describe each species so minutely as to enable a classifier to assign to it its place among the families and genera of fishes.

This work has all been done for us by previous explorers, and the time has now fully arrived that we can afford to start from general principles, and lead the student by natural stages to recognize apart the several species. In short, it is now possible, thanks to the painstaking labours of our predecessors, to attempt a popular work on this subject without incurring the danger of running into serious error.

So much for the difficulties; but the study of Ichthyology has one great advantage, which is this. Fishes are very slightly subject to variations at different ages and under different circumstances. With birds one species may have a plumage for winter use, and a different dress in summer, or the young may have very little resemblance to the old bird, or the male to the female. With insects the larval and pupal forms have to be studied as well as the mature insect, and similar uncertainty occurs in other classes of the animal kingdom. With fish this is rarely the case; the sexes hardly ever differ in appearance, and the young of most species possess all the characteristics of the full-grown fish (there are exceptions of course to this as to most general rules). It is as easy, for instance, to identify a mahaseer of two inches in length, as one of four feet.

In India the study has special advantages. Hardly anywhere in India are specimens not obtainable at any time of year, and in great variety: each tank or stream has an interest of its own, and if a person is unable to go out and collect for himself, it is always easy to employ fishermen, who bring specimens to the house where they can be examined at leisure.

A matter of great interest connected with the

fresh-water fishes of the Indian Peninsular is the geographical distribution of species and groups. India affords a splendid example of a well defined region. The great range of the Himalaya cuts it off most completely from the rest of Asia, and the sea being the boundary on almost every other side, it is manifest that no fresh-water species, as such, can at the present time have communication with other countries. Hence very few truly fresh-water species that are found in India occur in other countries; a few only extend to Burmah and the Malay Archipelago on the one side, or to Afghanistan on the other; one species, frequenting mountain streams, is found as far west as Syria. This subject will be further discussed when describing the Genera and Species in detail.

CHAPTER II.

ON CLASSIFICATION.

THE Fishes form one of the Great CLASSES of the Animal Kingdom.

They are divided by the latest authors, first into six SUB-CLASSES, as follows:—

I. TELEOSTEI, or fishes with a complete bony skeleton, which includes all the most perfectly organised forms; by far the greater number of existing fishes are included in this sub-class, among them all the species that we are concerned with in this book.

II. DIPNOI, of which only two species are known.

III. GANOIDEI, in which are the sturgeons, and a few other forms.

IV. CHONDROPTERYGII. Fishes with a cartilaginous skeleton, which includes all the sharks and rays.

V. CYCLOSTOMATA. "Round-mouthed," or sucking-fishes, including the lampreys and their allies.

VI. LEPTOCARDII. Only one species known.

The next division is into ORDERS.

We need only concern ourselves here with the first sub-class or Teleostei. These are divided into six ORDERS.

1. First come those fishes of which the perch may be taken as a type. They have usually a number of sharp spines forming part of the fin on the back, and some of the other fins.

They are termed ACANTHOPTERYGII, (spiny-finned.)

2. The second order contains fishes much resembling the first, differing from them only by an anatomical peculiarity of the lower bones of the throat, which is not to be wondered at when we learn that they call themselves ACANTHOPTERYGII PHARYNGOGNATHI.

3. The third order have all their fin rays soft and flexible, such as the cod-fish and the soles, they are termed ANACANTHINI, "without spines."

4. The fourth order contains the greater number of fresh-water fishes, and is the one with which we shall be chiefly concerned. The fishes of this order have frequently one strong bony ray in front of the back fin, but the remaining rays of that fin are soft and branched. They are termed PHYSOSTOMI.

5. The fifth order LOPHOBRANCHII } are unimportant.
6. The sixth order PLECTOGNATHI }

The next division to be considered is that of *Families*, and these form perhaps the most important and natural of the groups into which fishes can be divided; each family forms generally a well defined congregation, so that in the majority of cases there is little difficulty in deciding the family to which a fish belongs. Some species there are certainly which lie on the borderland between one family and another, as must be expected, but these cases are comparatively few.

Some families inhabit the salt water exclusively; some are confined, as, for instance, the Cyprinidæ, to fresh waters. Some, as the Salmonidæ, are only found in the temperate regions of the Northern Hemisphere, being apparently unable to pass the heated waters of the tropics, while others are only found in tropical regions, being unable to exist in the colder climates. Other families again have representatives in all parts of the globe.

In the fresh waters of India two families are most plentifully represented, viz., the Cyprinidæ, or carp family, and the Siluridæ. The latter are easily recognised by wanting scales.

The Ophiocephalidæ, or Snake-headed fishes, have also a good many species in India; and many other families are represented by one or two species, but perhaps nine-tenths of the fishes that are usually met with belong to one or other of the two first-mentioned families.

(As an example among large animals of what constitutes a *family*, we may instance the Family Bovidæ, which includes in it, sheep, goats, oxen, antelope, bison, etc., each of these forming a separate *genus.*)

The next division is that of the Genera.

A genus may be defined, roughly, as a group of fishes, which closely resemble one another in all important details of their structure, and differ from all other genera in one or more essential points; it may contain only one species, or it may contain a very great number; the genus Barbus, for example, in Günther's Catalogue, numbers over 160 species.

It is, as may be supposed, a difficult matter to decide what points are of sufficient importance to constitute a genus, and as almost every writer on the subject considers himself qualified to form his own opinion, and to bestow names of his own choosing, the result is a most embarrassing confusion.

It must be borne in mind that the members of each separate family have a tendency to vary in certain respects, and to remain constant in certain other points.

The Siluridæ, for instance, are eminently variable as to their teeth, the Cyprinidæ, on the other hand, vary very slightly in this respect.

Hence it is easy to understand that a slight difference in the number of their teeth between two Cyprinoid fishes would suffice to indicate that they belong to different genera, whereas a much greater difference might exist between the teeth of two Siluroid fishes who belong to one and the same genus; in their case it might only show that they were distinct species.

It is useful to remember that the first scientific

name of a plant or animal is the name of the genus. The second, distinctive, or specific name is frequently nothing but an adjective. Thus, for instance, "Barbus immaculatus," the "unspotted barbel," denotes a fish of the genus Barbus. The name of the genus is thus a kind of surname. Thus it happens that when an author sees fit to alter the classification adopted by previous writers, and to place a fish in a different genus, he at the same time alters the name of the fish itself. The consequence is, that the same fish may be described in four or five books by as many different names.

A most valuable aid to the study of Ichthyology is the British Museum descriptive Catalogue of Fishes, by Dr. Albert Günther, in 8 vols., in which the whole subject is treated in a comprehensive and masterly manner, and where all the names by which every known fish has been described by different authors is given, that specific name under which it was first described being accepted as the name of the fish, according to the recognised rule.

It is most devoutly to be hoped that future writers will endeavour, so far as possible, to follow the classification therein given, every deviation from which only tends to land us in a state of prægüntherite confusion.

(N.B. Vols. V. and VII. of Günther's work, containing the Families Siluridæ and Cyprinidæ, are those most particularly interesting to the Indian student.)

A *Species* is, as it were, the unit of which all groups are formed. All the individuals of a species resemble each other both in structure and habits; they breed freely together, and their progeny resemble themselves.

The only difference between individuals of a species is that due to sex; and among fishes there is seldom any perceptible outward distinction between the male and the female. A species may be either considered as a separate creation, or, in the view which is now more generally held, as a stereotyped variety of some older form. The latter view binds the entire organised creation into an harmonious system. Giving reins to our imagination, we discern, in the mind's eye, the various *orders* as vast branches of some primæval form of fathomless antiquity, each in process of time, as they increased and multiplied and scattered themselves in various climates, giving rise to divergent groups varying one from another, which we now rank as *families*; these again splitting up into *genera*, and each genus dividing into few or many separate forms which we call *species*.

There is little difficulty, with fishes at any rate, in discriminating one species from another (if we only have a sufficient number of specimens of each kind to compare together).

It is certainly quite conceivable that two species should exist, bearing the most perfect resemblance one to the other, in the minutest particulars, and yet quite distinct. It is possible to imagine that two forms which differed from each other ages ago should have thrown off convergent branches, so that the descendants of each, becoming more and more like each other, should now be undistinguishable apart. They would still, nevertheless, be distinct species, and would neither consort nor breed together. However, though theoretically imaginable, such cases do not practically occur; the developments of nature are infinite, and, however closely some forms may resemble others, there is always some point or other, if we only look close enough, which serves to distinguish each species apart.

A difficulty somewhat similar does, however, occur practically in dealing with groups. Groups perpetually inosculate with one another, and species may be found which seem in certain respects more nearly allied to other groups than the one to which they really belong. In these cases we have to discriminate between real and apparent affinities, and hence arise frequently differences of opinion between different systematists.

The more perfect our classification becomes, and the closer we follow nature in grouping such species as we are acquainted with, by so much the less are we troubled with wayward forms which seem to belong neither to one genus or another, but to possess affinity with two or more.

It must be remembered that we have at best but scanty material with which to build up the scheme of nature. We can observe the species of to-day, but many links are wanting, many forms must have died out to make room for the present ones.

Thus it sometimes happens that one single species is so far removed from its nearest allies that naturalists have to place it alone in a distinct family from all other species. Consequently there seem to be many blanks left in the series, the intermediate forms may be unknown to us, or else the existing form may be the only one that survives out of a large group, the remainder of which have become extinct.

We have seen that when two species that are really distinct are placed before us, and we are able to compare them critically one with the other, there is seldom any difficulty in discriminating between them. There is sometimes difficulty in knowing what group a fish belongs to; this is generally in consequence of the imperfection of our classification, and becomes less in proportion as our genera form natural groups.

There is, however, often a difficulty with fishes that in reality are of the same species, either they may have been described by different authors under distinct names, and each author may have laid stress on different points: in this case by comparing the descriptions alone, it is impossible to be certain if the fishes are the same or different: or else the species may be variable in itself, which often happens when it has a large geographical range, specimens from one locality differing from those of another, or the same individual appearing different at different times, according to the food it is living on, the kind of water it is inhabiting, or the season of the year.

Herein lies the great value of a large and carefully

arranged museum; collectors who discover and describe a new species, ought invariably to deposit type specimens in a museum where they will always be available for reference and comparison.

The necessity for this becomes at once apparent if we look at a work like the British Museum Catalogue.

Take the common Dace, for instance, Leuciscus vulgaris; it has been described under about 25 different names by various authors, and these on comparison all proved to refer to one and the same species!

Or take an Indian species, Discognathus lamta; this has been described under at least 20 names. It is a species that has a very wide geographical range, being found as far west as Palestine, and is liable to local variation.*

On the whole, therefore, in deciding between two specimens, are they varieties of the same species, or different? the safest rule seems to be as follows:—

Do they differ in only one respect, and is that a point with regard to which the individuals of that particular genus are usually inclined to be variable? In this case, the chances are that they belong to the same species, of which one or the other may be a local variety.

Fishes that have been long kept in confinement, or exposed to unnatural conditions are eminently liable to variation.

* The reason for the wide range of Discognathus lamta seems to be that it is a species living in rapid hill streams among the rocks and boulders; mountain ranges would thus, so long as they did not rise above the snow level, present little or no impediment to its spreading, as they do to species inhabiting the plains only.

On the other hand, if the two fishes really belong to different species, we will generally be able to find several points of difference; in fact the more carefully we study them the greater number of distinctions will be found.

Between two varieties there is an apparent difference, but no real distinction.

Between two species there may be a strong apparent similarity, but there is a real divergence in numerous respects of which we can usually discover more than one, at any rate, by careful scrutiny.

It must not be imagined that, because some species are variable, therefore a species as such has no definite existence. True, the species of to-day may be different from what they will be a thousand or a million years hence; some may have become extinct, others may have given birth to many new species, all varying from the original, but at any one time such species as exist are actual and clearly defined entities. In this they may be compared to the words in a language, derived from remote roots, constantly varying in the course of ages, yet each separate and distinct at any given time from all other words. In the same way as with species, words may appear similar and yet be widely different, or they may seem very distinct in outward appearance and yet be radically the same in point of fact.

This argument, it may be observed, does not imply the acceptance of the Doctrine of Evolution. It assumes variability of species, which is a fact proved by observation, but not of necessity the evolution of all forms from one, or from a few roots, which theory requires stronger evidence than is yet, or perhaps ever will be forthcoming, to make it certain.

CHAPTER III.

ON DISTRIBUTION.

As regards the Geographical Distribution of Genera, we find, among fresh-water fishes, that the *Genera* are confined within much narrower limits than are the *Families*.

To take a few instances.

Genus Barbus. Temperate and tropical parts of the Old World—Europe, Asia, Africa, East Indian Archipelago.

Genus Labeo. Tropical regions—Africa, and the East Indies, Java, Syria.

Genus Discognathus. Mountain streams, Syria, Persia, India, Ceylon.

Genus Crossochilus. East Indies, Java and Sumatra.

Genus Sclerognathus. North America and North China.

Genus Cyprinus. Temperate parts of Europe and Asia.

Genus Schizothorax. Mountain streams, Cashmere, and Afghanistan.

Genus Leuciscus. Temperate and Arctic Regions, Europe, N. America, Persia, Anatolia.

Genus Barilius. India, East Africa, River Nile.

The Cyprinidæ, being exclusively fresh-water fishes, and also being very numerous, and containing several large genera, are well adapted to elucidate this subject.

We find some genera that are frequenters of temperate and cold climates, and others that can only exist in tropical climates. The genus Leuciscus, for instance, is spread over the North of Europe and North America, not extending into Indian waters.

The genus Labeo, on the other hand, is found in tropical Africa and the East Indies only.

Some genera are confined to North America, occasionally spreading, as in genus Sclerognathus, into China *viâ* N.E. Asia. The large genus Barbus is found all over Europe, Asia, and Africa, but does not occur in America.

Most of the genera that inhabit the continent of India, extend also to the East Indian Archipelago, Java, and Sumatra.

Those Indian genera that inhabit mountain streams, such as Discognathus and Schizothorax, are also found in Afghanistan and Persia, but there seems no community between the fishes of India, and those of Northern Asia. The snowy ranges of the Himalayas seem to present an impassable barrier.

The range of species is much more closely restricted than that of genera. As before remarked, very few species that occur in India are to be found elsewhere, though most of the Indian species are met with all over the Indian continent. There are a few local species; some that are found only in Assam, some only in the Himalayan streams, some only in the streams of the Neilgherry hills in Madras, and so on, but these are generally species that live in rapid hill streams; those that inhabit still water, tanks, and the larger rivers of the plains are to be met with all over India.

A number of interesting questions suggest themselves in connection with this subject. How can a fish, take, for instance, Rasbora daniconius, have spread from India to the islands of the Eastern Archipelago, or *vice versâ?* Does this point to a time when these islands were connected with the main land? If this question is to be answered in the affirmative, we have here data for inferring the comparative antiquity of this species, as it is evident that it must have existed before the separation of these islands from the main land took place, and cannot have undergone any perceptible variation since that time.

Again, take a genus, Labeo, for instance, of which some species are confined to India, while others closely allied are found in Africa. This is essentially a tropical genus, which fact accounts for its not spreading northwards into Europe, but it would seem as if the relative positions of land and sea must have been different from what they are now in far distant ages, while the present species of Labeo must apparently have sprung into existence since that time, as some species are now confined to India, and others to Egypt.

There are several isolated waters in different parts of India, which it would be interesting to examine carefully and to note the species of fish to be found in them.

The lake at Nynee Tal is a good example; it is a large piece of water at a height of 6000 feet, having only one outlet, from which the surplus water escapes down a series of cascades, up which no fish could possibly make its way. Some fishes have been imported into the lake, I believe, from below, but it would be very interesting to know what species inhabit it naturally, and if they are the same as are to be found in the streams below.

Again, in the Khasia hills, the southern face of the plateau, overlooking the Sylhet district, breaks off very suddenly, and the streams are precipitated over the edge from a height of 3000 or 4000 feet, forming waterfalls of several hundred feet at a time. Unfortunately, in this case, the natives have a habit of poisoning the streams, so that there are very few fish of any kind to be found on the plateau.

However, there is one little species very common at Cherrapoonjee, and curiously enough it seems to be very closely allied, if not identical with a species (Danio neilgherriensis) that occurs in the streams on the Neilgherry hills, which are far away. It does not, so far as I am aware, occur in the streams at the foot of the Khasia hills; at any rate, it is not common in them, while of numerous kinds that are met with below the ridge, one can find no trace in the streams above.

Much patient and careful investigation would be required before any definite conclusion could be arrived at in cases like these. I merely mention the facts as they occur to me, in order to show what interesting inquiries present themselves in prosecuting the study of Natural History, It need not be merely a pedantic affair of long names and formulæ, nor is there any absolute necessity for making it a cause of jealousy and bickering; on the contrary, it may be made a delightful and perennial source of amusement and interest, while out of it spring problems which elevate the study to the rank of a science, and connect it in close relationship with Geography, Meteorology, and Astronomy.

Such problems as hinge on the geographical distribution of species cannot be answered off-hand; they necessitate a great amount of patient observation; our knowledge as yet is very imperfect; in fact, we may say that what we now know is only sufficient to indicate the lines on which further inquiries can be most usefully made. There is plenty still to be done: of hardly one single district or river of India can we say that we know what fishes are, and (which is more important still) what kinds are not to be found there. Of hardly any species do we know its exact range, or are we sufficiently acquainted with its food and habits, to be able to account for the reason of its occurring in one stream rather than in another.

There are are two institutions which are calculated to afford much assistance in this study. I mean museums and aquaria. The first to be of any real use should be a public affair; the second, even on a small scale, in a private house, is of great value. Some day perhaps every province, or even every district of India, may have its museum containing specimens of all objects of Natural History indigenous therein, well arranged and properly looked after. (Only on this condition are they of any use, otherwise they become mere curiosity shops.) It would be an immense boon to the collector to be able to deposit his specimens in the nearest museum, if he knew that they would be duly examined, and, if new or interesting, described, or forwarded to the British Museum as the case might require. This is perhaps too much to hope for just now. Meanwhile the aquarium as a means of study is available to all of us on a small scale. It is in itself a source of much interest, besides being ornamental; it need not be a large or expensive affair—one or more glass globes, or even lamp shades, enable one to watch the habits of a great variety of the smaller species, which abound in every tank and pond.

And very little trouble or attention is required, the main point being not to put too many fish into one vessel, and not to allow the sun to shine upon the water, or else it soon gets thick and green. If properly arranged, with a few sprigs of water weed growing in it, the water will remain clear and bright for months.

It would be a great boon if a fresh-water aquarium on a large scale, similar to the marine aquaria that have lately been established at home, at Brighton and other places, could be set up in India. The great variety and beauty of the Indian fishes would then be appreciated; and valuable results might ensue in relation to the importance of fish as a food supply, a subject which Dr. Day has lately been investigating on behalf of Government.

CHAPTER IV.

DESCRIPTIONS OF SOME OF THE PRINCIPAL FAMILIES OF FISH.

I PROPOSE here to notice very briefly some of the most important and best known of the Families, previous to the consideration of those species in detail, with which we are more especially concerned.

Gasterosteidæ. Sticklebacks.

These are eccentric little fishes, inhabiting both fresh and salt waters; being found plentifully in England, their habits have been well observed and described by Couch, Yarrell, Wood, and other authors. Some of the species build nests for the protection of their eggs, and are very pugnacious in their defence.

Percidœ. Perch.

This is a very extensive family, inhabiting fresh and salt water, in all climates. The common Perch of England, the Black Basse of America, are examples. In Indian seas the family is represented by several genera. Serranus, Genyoroge, Mesoprion, etc., and Ambassis, the latter are small fishes, and are found in fresh water.

Pristipomatidæ.

These form a large family, mostly found in salt water, in the tropical regions. They are large, handsome fishes. Several genera, for instance, Therapon, Diagramma, Datnoides, etc., are represented in Indian seas.

Mullidæ.

That delicious fish, the Red Mullet, belongs to this family, it inhabits European seas.

Squamipinnes. "Scaly-finned fishes."

This family consists mostly of bright-coloured fishes, with bodies very deep in comparison to their length, and very narrow, with small mouths, inhabiting tropical seas. The Chœtodons, and Holocanthi, form good Indian examples. This family is distinguished by the scales extending over a large portion of the dorsal and anal fins.

Triglidæ. Gurnards.

Are a large family, containing a great variety of fishes of extraordinary shapes and coloration, mostly marine. The British Gurnards, Bullheads, Miller's thumb, the Indian Dactylopterus, or Flying Gurnard, Pteröis, Scorpœna, and Platycephalus, are included in this group.

Trachinidæ.

The fishes of this family are generally of a long

shape, and usually inhabit salt water, the European Sting fishes are armed with poisonous spines. The Indian Sillago is much esteemed for eating.

Sciænidæ.

This family has several representatives, generally of a large size, in the Indian seas, belonging to the genera, Sciæna, Collichthys, Corvina, etc. Some species, such as the Maigre, have the power of producing a drumming or grunting sound beneath the surface of the water.

Polynemidæ.

The delicious Mangoe fish, Polynemus paradiseus, and P. indicus, are good examples of this family. The former has seven, and the latter five filiform appendages below the pectoral fin.

Scombridæ. The Mackerel family.

Are well known on account of their importance as an article of food. They are marine fishes. The family includes the common Mackerel, the Tunny, the Albacore, the Bonito, the Pilot-fish, the Remora or Sucking-fish, the John Dory, and the Coryphene, or dolphin of sailors.

Carangidæ.

Are deep narrow fish, represented in Indian seas by the genus Caranx (containing the Cobbler-fish), Equula, and others.

Ziphiidæ, or Swordfish.

Are well known on account of their bony weapon,

specimens of which may be seen in most museums and curiosity collections.

Gobiidæ. The Gobies.

Carnivorous fishes, living at the bottom, in fresh and salt waters of temperate and tropical regions.

Gobius giuris is a very common Indian Example.

Bleniidæ. The Blennies.

Are a most ferocious lot of little fishes; they reside mostly on or near the bottom, and include the Sea Wolf, the Shanny, Jumper-fish, etc.; some of the species are remarkable for producing their young alive, and not depositing eggs.

Acronuridæ.

Herbivorous fishes, found in tropical seas, the tail is usually provided with a sharp spine.

Nandidæ.

Carnivorous fishes, of which the sub-family Nandina, including the genera Badis, Nandus, and Catopra, inhabit the fresh waters of the East Indies.

Labyrinthici.

Fresh waters of the East Indies, and South Africa.

These fishes are remarkable for the length of time they are able to live without water, their gills being especially adapted to breathe the air direct. Even when in water they are obliged to ascend to the surface constantly to breathe, otherwise they are soon drowned. Anabas scandeus, and Trichogaster fasciatus are common Indian examples.

Mugilidæ. Grey Mullet.

Are found in the fresh waters, and near the coasts of all temperate and tropical regions.

Ophiocephalidæ. "Snake-headed fishes."

Are well represented in the Indian rivers and tanks. They can exist without water for a considerable time, and are carnivorous in their habits.

Fistularidæ.

Have long slender snouts, like the stems of tobacco-pipes, they are found in the Indian Ocean.

Mastacembelidæ. Spiny eels.

These fishes are found in Indian fresh waters.

Labridæ.

Marine fishes, inhabiting temperate and tropical regions, they are remarkable for the great beauty of their coloration; some species of Labrus, found off the British coasts, are known as Wrasse; they feed chiefly on shell-fish.

Gadidæ.

The Cod-fish is a fine specimen of this family, in which are also included the Haddock, Whiting, Pollack, and Hake.

Pleuronectidæ. Flat-fishes.

Should more correctly be termed deep, or thin fishes, as in truth they rest on one side, some species on the left and some on the right side. Their peculiarity consists in their carrying both eyes on one side of the head, the right or left side, whichever is uppermost; and it is remarkable that when young their eyes are placed as in other fish, but become twisted round as they grow larger. The upper side of these fish is always dark, and the under side light coloured.

The Sole, Turbot, Brill, and Flounder are English examples of this family, and some species are also found in India.

Siluridæ.

This is one of the largest families of fish known, and includes no less than 114 genera, more than any other family; they are inhabitants of the fresh waters of temperate and tropical regions, some of the species frequenting the sea also, and are numerously represented in India. They are hardly known in Europe, one species only being found in the Eastern parts of Europe. They are without scales, and have fleshy tendrils or feelers attached to their mouths. Also frequently a gristly, or adipose fin on the back, placed behind the usual rayed dorsal fin.

Scopelidæ.

Are deep sea fishes, among them is included Harpodon nehereus, the "Bombay duck," a well-known delicacy, when dried and smoked, in India. They have an adipose fin like the preceding family, but no barbels, and sometimes are covered with scales, entirely, or partially.

Salmonidæ. The Salmon family.

Are well known in Europe and North America; it includes the Salmon, Trout, Greyling and Smelt.

There are no representatives of this family in India, nor indeed anywhere south of the Equator, excepting that lately Salmon and Trout have been naturalized in Australia and New Zealand. They have an adipose fin, but no barbels, and are covered with scales.

Esocidæ.

This family includes the English Pike, a carnivorous and most voracious fish.

Scombresocidæ. Mackerel-pike,

Include the Gar-fish, Belone vulgaris, a long, queer-shaped fish which is often taken in mackerel nets; also a fish very closely similar, Belone cancila, which is found in Indian rivers.

The genus Exocetus, or Flying-fish, belongs to this family.

Cyprinidæ. Carp family.

This family is perhaps the largest in actual numbers of all the families; it contains 107 genera, and being confined to the fresh waters of the Old World and North America, the members of it are well known.

By far the greater number of Indian fresh-water fish belong to this family. The Carp, Barbel, Roach, Bream, etc., are English representatives.

They have scales, and frequently barbels, but no adipose fin.

Clupeidæ. Herring family.

Are well known for their excellence as food.

The Herring, the fry of which is the Whitebait, the Pilchard or Sardine, the Shad, Anchovy, and Sprat, in Europe, and the Hilsa or Indian Shad, in India, are examples. The last named ascends the large rivers hundreds of miles for breeding purposes.

Notopteridæ.

Are queer shaped fishes, found in the fresh waters of the East Indies and West Africa. There are only five species known of this family, of which two are Indian.

Gymnotidæ.

Eel-like fishes found in fresh waters in Tropical America. The electric eel belongs to this family.

Symbranchidæ.

Eel-like fish of the Tropics, the genera Amphipnous and Symbranchus occur in India.

Murænidæ. Eels.

Are found everywhere in fresh and salt water; they are not, numerous, however, in India.

Gymnodontes.

This family have the jaws formed like a beak, in two, three, or four bony pieces. Some species of Tetradon are found in India, and are queer looking little fish. They have a trick when handled of inflating themselves with air, till they form a complete ball.

Acipenseridæ. The Sturgeons.

These fish have five rows of bony plates running

the whole length of the body, they grow to a large size.

Chimæridæ.

Are very extraordinary looking fishes, very brilliantly coloured, inhabiting the seas of the North and South Hemisphere remote from the Tropics.

The sub-order SELACHOIDEI, or Sharks, include the families:

Scylliidæ, or Dog-fish.

Carchariidæ, including the Blue Shark, Hammer-headed Shark, etc.

Lamnidæ, including the terrible White Shark.

Spinacidæ, *Rhinodontidæ*, *Notidanidæ*, *Heterodontidæ*, *Rhinidæ*, and *Pristiophoridæ*.

The Sub-Order BATOIDEI contains the

Pristidæ, or Saw-fish.

Torpedinidæ, or Electric fish.

Rajidæ, *Trygonidæ*, and *Myliobatidæ*, which comprise the various Rays, Skates, Sting-rays, Horned-rays, etc.

Petromyzontidæ. Lampreys.

Are long-bodied snake-like fishes, with mouths formed into suckers by which they cling to stones, and a row of holes for breathing on each side of the throat. They live both in salt and fresh water.

Cirrostomi.

Only one species, the Amphioxus, is known of this family, the lowest form in the scale of development among fishes. In fact, it can hardly be ranked as a vertebrate animal, as it appears to possess neither bones nor any of the usual organs of sense.

CHAPTER V.

DESCRIPTIONS OF THE SPECIES AND GENERA INHABITING THE FRESH WATERS OF THE INDIAN CONTINENT.

In these descriptions I shall not altogether follow the order of sequence observed in strictly scientific works, but I shall attempt to describe first such fishes as are most commonly met with, and most easily procured for purposes of identification. It will be found that when once acquaintance has been formed with the peculiarities of a few species, it becomes much easier to recognise any other kinds, and to hit off at once the points of difference or resemblance they may possess.

Neither shall I attempt to give a full scientific description of each species, for such as wish to devote much time to the study more ambitious works are procurable. My aim will be to indicate some one or more peculiarities of each species by which it may be quickly identified, preferably such outward peculiarities as the number of the scales, or of the fin rays, and so on, that can easily be observed. It must not therefore be supposed that the points I here notice are in all cases the ones with regard to which the classification of the fish has been decided.

It is necessary to know the names of the fins, and the signification of the other terms used in these descriptions.

By referring to Plate 10 it will be seen that the fin on the back of the fish is termed the "Dorsal fin." There may be one or two dorsal fins; of which the hindmost may be an adipose, or gristly fin, without rays.

The fin opposite to the dorsal, on the lower surface of the body, is termed the Anal fin.

The fin at the end of the tail is the Caudal fin. (N.B. The tail of a fish is understood to be that part of the body between the anal and the caudal fins, it is a mistake to call the fin itself the tail).

These comprise the vertical fins, the remaining fins are disposed in pairs, and answer to the four limbs of a quadruped. The upper pair are termed the Pectoral fins, the lower pair are called the Ventral fins.

In taking measurement the following rule has been observed:—By the "total length" I understand the length in a straight line from the end of the snout to the base of the caudal fin; that is to say, the total length not including the caudal fin. This affords a better standard of comparison, as the fin is frequently damaged, or may vary slightly in length, than if the fin were included.

The length of the head is from the end of the snout to the hinder edge of the gill cover, in a straight line, not measured round the corner.

The depth of body is taken at the deepest part, usually just in front of the dorsal fin.

By "Scales," is meant the number of scales in the length of the body, from the gill cover to the end of the tail. There will usually be found a line of pores running along the side; this is called the lateral line, and when it runs straight along the middle of the side, the scales may conveniently be counted along it. Sometimes however it is interrupted, or bent suddenly downwards, or wanting altogether. "Tr." (=transverse,) means the number of rows of scales from the back to the belly; it is as well to count these in three divisions, viz. from the back to the lateral line, from the line to the ventral fin, and from the ventral fin to the centre of the abdomen, thus 7+4+3.

The barbels may be variously placed.

If belonging to the nostril, they are termed nasal.

If at the end of the snout, rostral.

If under the chin, mandibular.

If on, or at, the corner of the upper jaw, maxillary.

FAMILY CYPRINIDÆ. (Günth. Cat. vol. vii.)

I take this Family first, as they are the most generally known, and everywhere procurable.

Geographical distribution. Fresh waters of the Old World and North America.

Description. This family is best recognised by the absence of any marked peculiarities. The gold carp is an example familiar to most people. The body is covered with scales, which do not extend on to the head. There is only one dorsal fin, of which the first two or three rays (counting from the head) are united, and form an unbranched ray, which is frequently bony and strong, and is sometimes toothed or serrated on the hinder edge. The remaining rays are soft and divided towards the free end, the last ray generally appears double, care must therefore be taken in counting the fin rays not to count this one twice over, as it is in fact only one ray. *They have no teeth in any part of their mouths.* The only teeth they possess are situated on a pair of bones in the throat, just beneath the gill-cover, these are termed Pharyngeal teeth, and may be in one, or in two, or in three series.

Char. No visible teeth. No adipose fin. Body covered with scales, head naked. Mouth frequently with barbels.

GENUS BARBUS.

This being the largest genus, I will take it first.

GEOGRAPHICAL DISTRIBUTION. Europe, Asia, and Africa.

DESCRIPTION. The species of this genus differ greatly in size, from the mahaseer, which has been known to grow to 80 or 100lb. in weight, to the minute *Barbus gelius* of an inch, or an inch and a half in length.

In appearance they also differ considerably, but the graduation being perfect from one end of the series to the other, they have all been included in one genus. They all possess a short dorsal and anal fin, the number of rays being Dorsal 3+8, Anal 7 or 8. These numbers are almost invariable, there may sometimes be one more or less. The number of scales varies from 20 to 47.

CHAR. The mouth opens forwards, the lips are clean, without fringes, or inner folds, or horny covering. The lateral line runs along the middle of the body and tail.

We may, for convenience, divide this large genus into three groups.

A. Species having four barbels.

B. Species having two barbels.

C. Species without barbels.

I

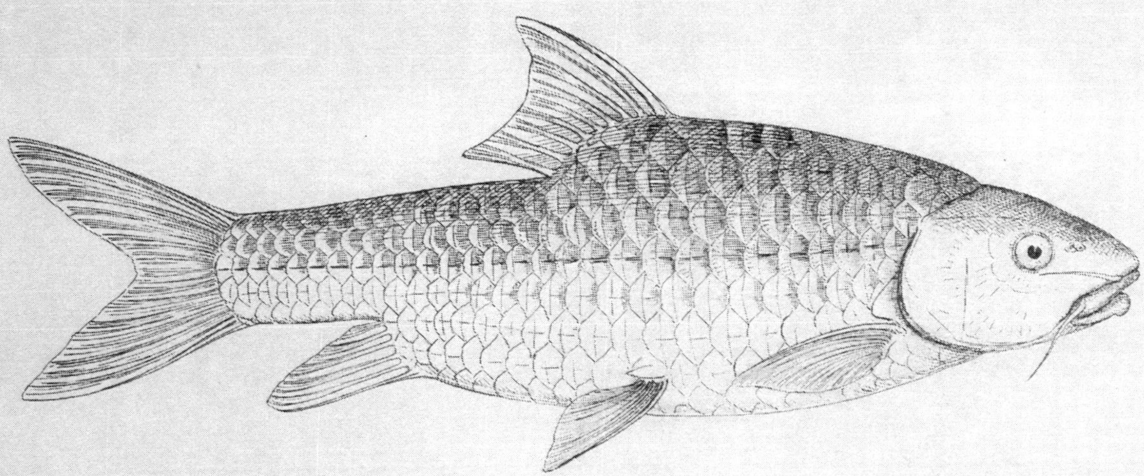

BARBUS MOSAL.

London: L. Reeve & Co

A. Species with four Barbels.

These we may further subdivide, according as the first long ray of the dorsal fin is (a) *strong and bony;* (b) *serrated on the inner edge;* or (c) *feeble and flexible.*

(a) *Principal ray of the dorsal fin osseous and strong.*

1. Barbus mosal. The Mahaseer.

This fish is to be found generally throughout India in rapid streams and deep pools, not far from hilly regions.

It is the fish best known to the Indian sportsman, as it grows to a large size, and will take a bait well; it has been known to exceed a hundred pounds in weight. It affords good sport, and fights gamely when hooked. Neither is it to be despised when on the table. So much has been written by various authors on the subject of the Mahaseer, that I need not here pause to describe its habits.*

Under the name of *Barbus mosal* I have included several varieties, which may perhaps deserve to be reckoned as distinct species.

There seem, however, as yet, to have been no sufficient differences pointed out by which to identify each variety separately with any amount of certainty, as they merge one into another, and show considerable variation among themselves. I have preferred therefore to place them all under one name, which includes the following varieties:—

* A most useful and interesting work on this subject, entitled 'The Rod in India' by H. S. Thomas, of the Madras Civil Service, was published at Mangalore in 1873.

Cyprinus { *Putitora*, *Mosal*, *Tor* } of Ham. Buchanan, the principal difference between which appears to lie in the shape of the head.

Barbus.	*Progeneius.* "Jhungha." Assam	of M'Clelland.
	Macrocephalus "Burapetea," Ass.	
	Megalepis. (= *Mosal*, H.B.)	

Here again the principal difference seems to be in the head. However, as two of these varieties are known to the natives of Assam by different names, there is reason to believe that they may really be distinct species.

Dr. Günther has given *Barbus macrocephalus* a separate place in his Catalogue, but remarks that it is at present a very doubtful species. The remainder he has placed together under the name of *Barbus mosal.*

Dr. Day considers *Barbus mosal* and *putitora* of Buchanan, and *macrocephalus* of M'Clelland, to be one species; and *B. tor*, and *B. progeneius*, he describes as a separate species under the name of *Barbus tor.* The difference between these two forms he states to consist in the latter having a pointed snout, the lower jaw being the shortest; mouth somewhat deeply cleft, lips thick and cartilaginous, with protruding lobes.

Barbus mosal, Günth.	*Barbus macrocephalus*,, M'C.	*Barbus mosal*, Day,
	Cyprinus putitora, H.B.	
	Cyprinus mosal, H.B.	
	Cyprinus tor, H.B.	*Barbus tor*, Day.
	Barbus progeneius, M'C.	

These fish vary so much, however, with regard to the apparent shape of their heads and the thickness of their lips, according to their age, the kind of stream they are living in, and the season of the year, that I think it safer at present to leave them under one name, although they may possibly turn out eventually to belong to two or more distinct species. I have found generally that those which are found in still water, or such as have been feeding chiefly on water weeds, and the larger specimens, have soft thick lips, more or less lobed, of which the upper has a tendency to project over the lower one, and to make the head appear more pointed. So far as I can make it out, the only reliable point seems to be the comparative length of the head.

In *Barbus mosal* the length of the head is contained $3\frac{3}{4}$ times in the total length (exclusive of the tail fin). In large individuals the proportion is nearer $3\frac{1}{2}$ times.

Counting the scales along the lateral line from the head to the caudal fin, there will usually be found to be about 26, sometimes one more or less. Counting diagonally downwards from the centre of the back, there will be found four series to the lateral line, and four more from the line to the centre of the belly. There are two entire series between the lateral line and the root of the ventral fin.

Char. Dorsal ray bony and strong. 25 to 27 scales along the lateral line, not more than two rows between the lateral line and the ventral fin.

Head contained $3\frac{1}{2}$ to $3\frac{3}{4}$ times in the total length.

2. Barbus hexastichus.

HABITAT. Assam and Himalayan streams. Grows to $2\frac{1}{2}$ feet in length = 10 or 12lb. weight.

CHAR. This fish differs from *Barbus mosal* in having a smaller head, the length of which is contained $4\frac{1}{2}$ times in the total length. Scales 24 to 28.

3. Barbus carnaticus.

HAB. Rivers along the base of the Neilgherries and the Wynaad range of hills. Reaches 25lb. weight.

CHAR. Head contained $4\frac{1}{2}$ times in the total length.
Scales 30 to 32 (Day).
" 25 to 29 (Günth.)

4. Barbus chilinoides.

HAB. Rivers of the Himalayas. 8 inches in length.

CHAR. Head contained 4 to $4\frac{1}{2}$ times in the total. Scales 32 to 35. Dorsal ray very stout.

5. Barbus himalayanus.

HAB. Ussun river, near Simla. Sylhet. 7 inches.

CHAR. Head contained $2\frac{2}{3}$ (?) times in the total. Scales 32 to 34. Dorsal ray moderately strong. Colour golden above, in the young a black mark behind the gill openings.

6. Barbus conirostris.

This fish is described by Dr. Day as *Barbus mysorensis*. I think it is perhaps better to adhere to Dr. Günther's name which has been, as it were, stereotyped in the Catalogue of the British Museum.

II

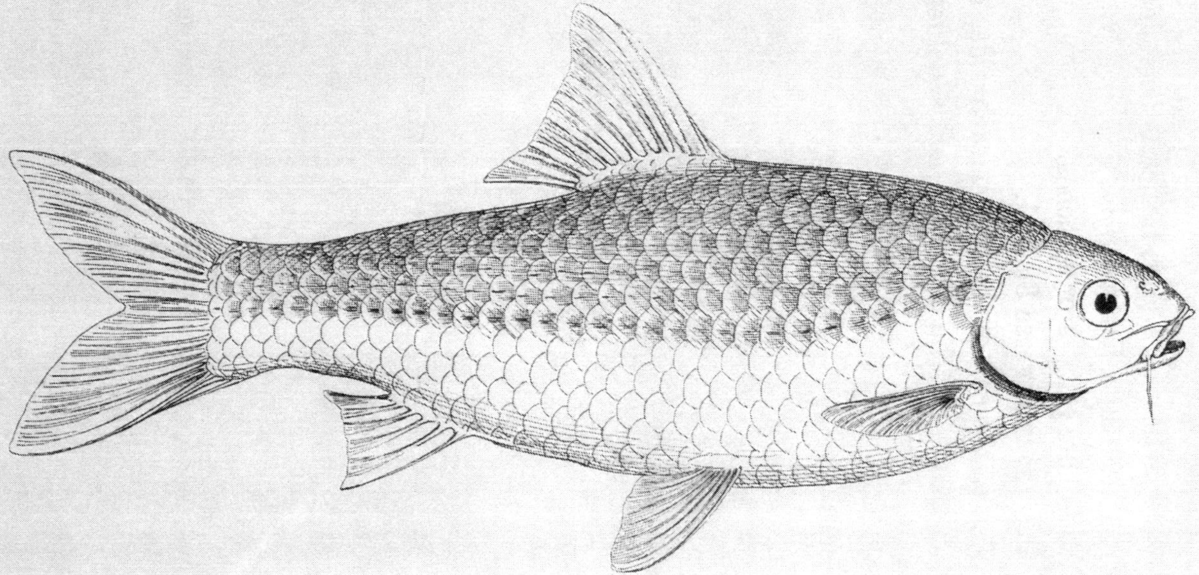

BARBUS SARANA.

London: L. Reeve & C°

14. **Barbus chagunio,** (*beavani*, Günth.)

It is an undecided question, whether the fish described by Buchanan under this name is identical with Gunther's *B. beavani*. As the distinction seems doubtful, I have preferred Buchanan's name for the present. This and other similar questions will doubtless be settled some day, by further investigation; it would be out of place to discuss them here.

Hab. Bengal. Attains 1½ feet in length, and is said to be good eating.

Char. Scales 44 to 47, transverse 11+11.

Six rows of scales between the lateral line and ventral fin.

15. **Barbus clavatus.**

Hab. Sikkim and base of Khasia Hills.

Char. Scales 42.

Head contained rather more than 4 times in total.

16. **Barbus sarana.**

The ray of the back fin is strong and finely serrated, the teeth on it are not large like those of the preceding species, and they lie in a double row. This is a very common fish, and liable to considerable variation in different localities.

Hab. Throughout India, grows up to 2 feet in length.

Char. Scales about 31, transverse 5 or 6+6 or 7.

3 or 4 rows between the lateral line and the ventral fin.

17. **Barbus immaculatus.**

This fish seems scarcely to differ from the preceding species, except that the number of the scales are slightly greater. It may possibly be a variety of *B. sarana.*

HAB. Himalayan streams, 10 or 12 inches.

CHAR. Scales 32 to 34.

18. **Barbus pinnauratus.**

HAB. R. Indus, Kurnool, and Malabar. 5 inches.

CHAR. Scales 27 to 29, transverse 6+5.

A dark spot on the side, about the 24th to the 28th scales along the lateral line.

19. **Barbus roseipinnis.**

HAB. Pondicherry. $4\frac{1}{2}$ inches.

CHAR. Scales 22.

Lower border of the caudal fin tinged with black.

(c). *The principal ray of the dorsal fin is flexible, and not serrated.*

20. **Barbus spinulosus.**

HAB. Found near Darjeeling, in Sikkim, a Himalayan region.

CHAR. Scales 32.

Head contained 4 times in the total length.

21. **Barbus pulchellus.**

HAB. Canara district, Madras. Length of one specimen, $17\frac{1}{2}$ inches.

CHAR. Scales 30, transverse $6+5\frac{1}{2}$. Four rows between the lateral line and the ventral fin.

22. Barbus melanampyx.

In Dr. Günther's Catalogue this species is named *B. arulius*. This name belongs however to a fish described by Dr. Jerdon, which, having only one pair of barbels, will be noticed presently. This one, with four barbels, would seem to be a distinct species.

HAB. The base of the Wynaad, Neilgherry, and Travancore Hills. A small species, rarely attaining 3 inches.

CHAR. Scales 20, transverse $3\frac{1}{2}+3\frac{1}{2}$.

23. Barbus thomassi.

HAB. South Canara. 18 inches.

CHAR. Scales 31. Dorsal rays 4+9.

$2\frac{1}{2}$ rows between the lateral line and the ventral fin. Dorsal fin edged with black; pectorals, ventrals, and anal fin stained.

24. Barbus lithopodos.

HAB. South Canara.

CHAR. Scales 38. $3\frac{1}{2}$ to 4 rows between the lateral line and the ventral fin.

COLOUR slaty; outer rays of the caudal fin, whitish.

B. SPECIES HAVING TWO BARBELS.

We now come to the second division of the genus Barbus, comprising those species with only one pair of barbels.

We can subdivide these also, for convenience sake, into

(a). *Species with a strong bony dorsal ray.*

(b). *Species with a soft flexible dorsal ray.*

There are no Indian species of this division (as yet known) with the dorsal ray serrated,

(a). *Species having a strong bony ray to the dorsal fin.*

25. **Barbus chola.**

HAB. Throughout India. 5 inches.

This fish is said to be bitter, and not good for food.

CHAR. Scales 26 or 27, transverse $5\frac{1}{2}+5$.

Head contained 4 times. Depth of body $2\frac{1}{3}$ times in the total length. Generally a dark mark on the base of the anterior rays of the dorsal fin, and a spot on the tail near the end of the lateral line.

26. **Barbus dorsalis.**

HAB. Madras and Mysore. "It does not attain a large size."

CHAR. Scales 24, transverse $4\frac{1}{2}+4$.

A black spot at the hinder portion of the base of the dorsal fin.

27. **Barbus thermalis.**

HAB. Mysore, Cachar. 3 inches.

CHAR. Scales 25, transverse $5\frac{1}{2}+5\frac{1}{2}$ (Day); or $5+4\frac{1}{2}$ (Günth).

According to Dr. Day, the lateral line is incomplete, extending only over 8 scales. A round black finger mark on the tail, near the base of the caudal fin.

28. **Barbus amphibius.**

HAB. Bombay and the Western coast. 6 inches.

CHAR. Scales 23, trans. $4\frac{1}{2}+4$.

Generally a black spot on the tail, near the base of the caudal fin. Lateral line complete.

29. Barbus lepidus.

This fish is almost exactly similar to Barbus filamentosus, the only exception being that the latter has no barbels. Dr. Day considers them as distinct species, and I have therefore shown them as such.

HAB. Western coast, and base of Neilgherries, also Ceylon. 6 inches.

CHAR. Scales 21.

COLOUR silvery white, with a deep black oval mark on the lateral line from about the 14th to the 18th scales. Caudal fin red, tipped with black. The branched rays of the dorsal fin are elongated in the adult fish.

30. Barbus parrah.

HAB. Malabar, Mysore, and Madras. 6 inches.

CHAR. Scales 25.

A dark bluish line along the side. Pectoral, ventral, and anal fins tinged with yellow. Dorsal and caudal fins dusky. A diffused black spot on the lateral line, from the 20th to the 22nd scale.

31. Barbus titius.

HAB. Bengal and Northern India. 5 inches.

CHAR. Scales 25.

A round black spot on the lateral line, behind the gill openings, and a second midway between the end of the anal and the base of the caudal fins. Dorsal and anal fins tipped with black, sometimes the upper half of the former stained darkish.

(b). *Species having a soft flexible ray to the dorsal fin.*

32. **Barbus kolus.**

HAB. Bombay, Deccan. 1 foot, or upwards.

CHAR. Scales 40 to 42, transverse 10+8. Dorsal rays 3 or 4+9.

33. **Barbus curmuca.**

Very similar to *Barbus kolus*, Dr. Day mentions what seems to be a local variety of this species, found in South Canara, which has a second pair of maxillary barbels.

HAB. Malabar, and Central Provinces.

CHAR. Scales 42, transverse 10+9.

Head contained 4 times, depth $3\frac{1}{3}$ times in the total.

Anal and caudal fins sometimes edged with black.

34. **Barbus denisonii.**

HAB. Hill ranges of Travancore. 6 inches.

CHAR. Scales 28. Two series between the lateral line and the ventral fin.

A longitudinal black band runs along the side from the snout to the base of the caudal fin, and above it a crimson band. An oblique black band runs across the caudal fin.

35. **Barbus arulius.** (Not Günther's.)

HAB. Neilgherry and Wynaad Hills. 4 inches.

CHAR. Scales 23.

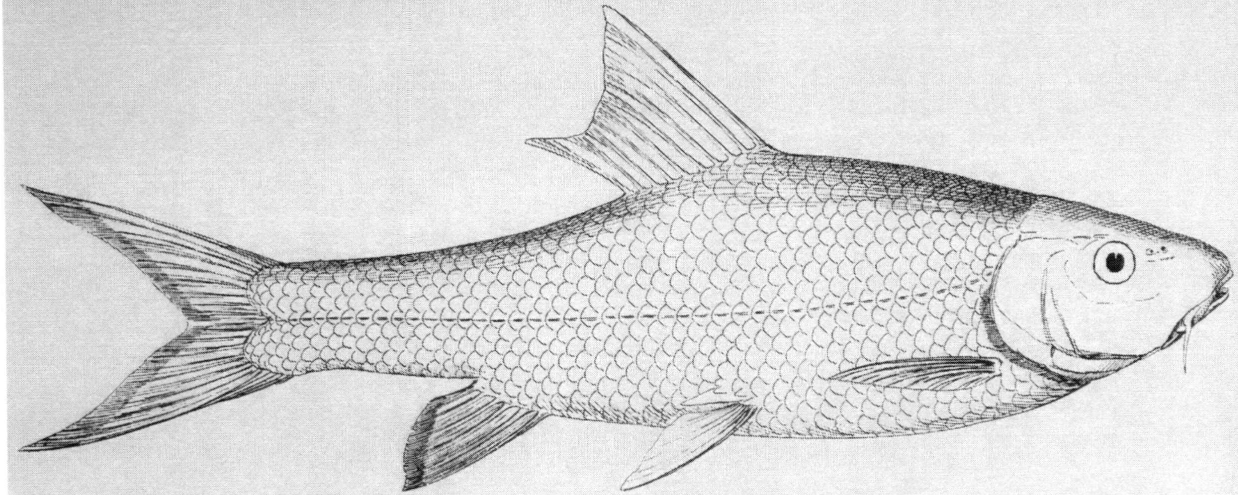

BARBUS CURMUCA.

London: L. Reeve & Co

Three transverse black bars down the sides. Dorsal and caudal fins edged with black.

36. **Barbus puckelli.**

HAB. Bangalore. 3 inches.

CHAR. Scales 24, transverse 4+3.

A scarlet stripe along the side. A deep black mark on the dorsal fin. An indistinct dark mark on the lateral line from the 19th to the 21st scales.

C. SPECIES WITHOUT BARBELS (Puntius).

We next come to the third division of genus Barbus, containing such species as have no barbels. They form a group of small fishes common all over India in ponds, and are generally brightly coloured.

Ham. Buchanan designated them as a separate division under the name of *Puntius*, but the series is so perfect between these and the species last described that it is impossible to draw the line of distinction except at those species that are without barbels, which are sometimes so minute as to make it difficult to ascertain their existence. It is even possible that some species, such as *Barbus lepidus* and *filamentosus*, the former with two barbels, the latter with none, or *Barbus titius* and *B. tetrarupagus*, may by further investigation turn out to be identical species which are liable to variation in this respect.

In this group the number of the scales is not of much value for identification, as, with the exception of *Barbus ambassis* with 36 scales, and *Barbus punja-*

bensis with 43, the greater number have about 25 scales along the lateral line.

The points to be looked at are the number and position of the dark spots with which most of them are ornamented, and the lateral line, which in some cases is incomplete, not running the whole length of the body

Like the first group, these may also be subdivided into

A. Species with a serrated dorsal ray.
B. Species with a smooth, bony dorsal ray.
C. Species with a soft, flexible dorsal ray.

A. Dorsal ray serrated.

37. **Barbus ambassis.**

Hab. Bengal and Madras. 3 inches.
Char. Scales 36.

A silvery streak along the side. A small spot at the base of the dorsal fin, and a mark on the tail. Lateral line incomplete.

38. **Barbus ticto.**

Hab. India generally. 4 inches.
Char. Scales 23.

A black spot on the side of the tail, immediately behind the anal fin. Another at the commencement of the lateral line. Fins often black.

Lateral line incomplete, ceasing after 6 or 8 scales.

39. **Barbus conchonius.**

Hab. Bengal and N. W. Provinces. 5 inches.

Char. Scales 25 or 26. Deeper in the form of the body than *B. ticto*. A round black spot on the tail, above the end of the anal fin, but not so far back as in *B. ticto;* sometimes a second spot near the head, more or less distinct.

Lateral line incomplete, ceasing after traversing 8 or 10 scales.

40. **Barbus phutonio.**

Hab. Bengal, Orissa, also Ceylon. 3 inches.

Char. Scales about 22. General colour reddish brown, two black bands pass downwards across the body, with two darkish marks between them, and one at the base of the caudal fin, forming five bands altogether.

Lateral line incomplete, extending 3 or 4 scales.

41. **Barbus gelius.**

Hab. Bengal, Central India. 1½ inches.

These minute fish are found in tanks and ponds, they swim in shoals among the water weeds, and, being brightly coloured, have a very pretty appearance.

Char. The bases of the dorsal and anal, and sometimes of the ventral fins are black. A black belt runs across the tail.

Lateral line incomplete, extending over 6 scales.

42. **Barbus pyrrhopterus.**

HAB. Assam.

CHAR. One dark spot on the lateral line, over the hinder end of the anal fin.

Lateral line complete.

43. **Barbus guganio.**

HAB. Assam. $1\frac{1}{2}$ inches.

CHAR. A small transparent, silvery species, without spots. Lateral line hardly perceptible.

44. **Barbus punctatus.**

HAB. Malabar. 3 inches.

CHAR. A black spot on the 20th and 21st scales. The anterior half of the fourth scale in the row below the lateral line, black. Dorsal fin with two rows of black spots, besides a short intermediate row. Lateral line complete.

B. DORSAL RAY STRONG, BUT NOT SERRATED.

45. **Barbus duvaucelii.**

HAB. Bengal.

CHAR. Scales 27.

A black spot just in front of the base of the caudal fin. Lateral line complete.

46. **Barbus stigma.** (*Sophore*, Günther.)

HAB. India generally.

This is a very common species. It is described in Günther's Catalogue under the name of *B. sophore*, which was the name given by Ham. Buchanan to a species nearly resembling this one, but with four minute barbels. Dr. Day states that a specimen answering this description exists in the Calcutta museum. *Stigma* is the name bestowed on the present species by Cuvier.

CHAR. It has a black spot on the tail, and one on the base of the dorsal fin. This last mark is sometimes wanting. Dr. Day states that at certain seasons it has a scarlet band along the side. Lateral line complete.

47. **Barbus modestus.**

HAB. Madras.

CHAR. No spots on the body, but a dark band across the dorsal fin. Lateral line complete.

48. **Barbus chrysopterus.**

HAB. Northern India, Assam.

M'Clelland describes this species as having no distinguishing spots. Dr. Day states that the ends of the dorsal, anal, and ventral fins are discoloured with minute dots, and a dark mark sometimes on the tail near the caudal fin. Lateral line complete.

49. **Barbus terio.**

HAB. Bengal. 3 or 4 inches.

CHAR. Scales 21.

A large black spot on the side of the body, above the front ray of the anal fin, sometimes a dark line from this spot to the end of the tail. In old individuals this spot becomes surrounded with a faint, light ring.

Lateral line incomplete, ceasing after the 3rd or 4th scale.

50. **Barbus tetrarupagus.**

HAB. Assam.

CHAR. One spot on the lateral line near the gills, and a second near the end of the line, on the tail.

51. **Barbus filamentosus.**

HAB. Southern and Western India. 6 inches.

Similar to *Barbus lepidus*, but without barbels. Body strongly compressed.

Dr. Day remarks, " a very curious change occurs in this fish immediately after death, the whole of its body becoming scarlet."

CHAR. The rays of the dorsal fin are extended into long filaments. Caudal fin red, tipped with black. A dark spot on the tail. Lateral line complete.

C. DORSAL RAY WEAK AND FEEBLE.

In this division there are five known species, which are easily distinguished apart, (not including *Leuciscus presbyter* of Cuvier, which is a doubtful species, insufficiently described). The lateral line in each of them is incomplete.

52. **Barbus vittatus.**

HAB. Mysore and Malabar. 1½ inches.

CHAR. Scales 20 to 22.

Generally with four black spots on each side, in the adult; one just in advance of the dorsal fin, one below its hinder end, one at the base of the caudal fin, and a fourth at the base of the anal; a black streak on the dorsal fin.

Lateral line incomplete, extending five scales.

53. **Barbus puntio.**

HAB. Bengal. 3 inches.

CHAR. Scales 23.

A wide black band encircles the free portion of the tail, and includes the tip of the anal fin. Dorsal fin orange tipped with black.

54. **Barbus cosuatis.**

HAB. Bengal. 2 or 3 inches.

CHAR. Scales 22 or 23.

A black mark on the top of the dorsal, and one on the front part of the anal fin.

55. **Barbus waageni.**

HAB. Salt Range, Punjab. $2\frac{1}{4}$ inches.

CHAR. Scales 23 or 24.

A black blotch on the 17th and 18th scales, posterior to the anal and dorsal fin. Lateral line ceases on the 7th scale.

56. **Barbus punjabensis.** 2 inches.

HAB. Punjab.

CHAR. Scales 43.

Fore part of dorsal fin black, and a spot on the tail. A bright silvery stripe along the side.

GENUS LABEO.

This is also a large genus, containing several fine species, such as the Roho, which are of considerable importance as an article of food.

It is essentially a tropical genus, being found only in tropical Africa and the East Indies.

The mouth is differently formed from that in the genus *Barbus.* It opens downwards, not forwards, being situated on the lower surface of the snout; the lips are thick and fleshy, one or both lips having an inner transverse fold, which is covered with a horny substance.

The barbels are small, either one pair or two, those at the corners of the mouth are more or less hidden in a groove.

The rays of the dorsal fin vary considerably. Dr. Günther has divided the Labeos into two genera, according as there are more than twelve rays or less than 13 in the dorsal fin, forming the latter into the genus Tylognathus.

I lately had brought to me about a dozen specimens of *Labeo ricnorhynchus*, of these about half had twelve rays (3+9), and the remainder thirteen (3+10), in the dorsal fin; in all other respects they were similar. As Dr. Günther himself acknowledges the divison to be an artificial one, it will perhaps be better for our purposes to class them all as *Labeo.*

The snout projects over the mouth, and has sometimes a lateral lobe, or projection, on each side, in form something similar to the nose of a dog.

CHAR. Mouth situated below the snout, lips thickened, and some times fringed, with a horny inner fold on one or both.

We can divide the genus *Labeo* into—

A. Species having a pair of barbels on the snout.

B. Species without barbels on the snout.

A. Species with Rostral Barbels.

1. Labeo nandina.

HAB. Bengal and Assam. 3 feet.

CHAR. This fish may be at once recognised by the length of its dorsal fin, which contains about 25 rays in all. It grows to a large size. "Two or three feet in length, and is a well-flavoured and wholesome fish." It has four barbels, two on the nose, and one at each corner of the mouth. The lips are thick, and both the upper and lower lips are fringed. There are from 40 to 44 scales along the lateral line.

Labeo macronotus is probably only a variety of this species.

2. Labeo fimbriatus.

HAB. Southern and Central India.

CHAR. Dorsal rays 18 to 21. Scales 44 to 47.

The head is small, and the lips are fringed.

(*Labeo leschenaultii* appears closely to resemble this species, but from specimens I have taken in the Nerbudda river intermediate in character, and showing considerable variation among themselves, I am in doubt as to their being distinct. I have therefore postponed the notice of *Labeo leschenaultii* to the appendix.)

It has four small barbels, of which the lower pair are the longest, the upper ones are sometimes absent in large specimens.

3. **Labeo calbasu.** "The Kala-bans."

HAB. Throughout India. Attains 4 feet.

This is a very common fish, it is dark in colour, generally blotchy, and very slimy; lips fringed.

CHAR. Dorsal fin rays, 3+14. Scales about 42.

4. **Labeo porcellus.**

HAB. Bombay.

CHAR. Very similar to *L. calbasu*, but having only 39 scales along the lateral line.

5. **Labeo nigrescens.**

HAB. Madras. 1½ feet.

CHAR. A small lateral lobe to the snout.

36 scales along the lateral line.

Colour deep brown, each scale with a black spot at the base. Fins black. Lower lip deeply fringed.

The following three species are remarkable for the small size of their scales. They have about 16 rays in the dorsal fin. They are not considered particularly good as food.

IV

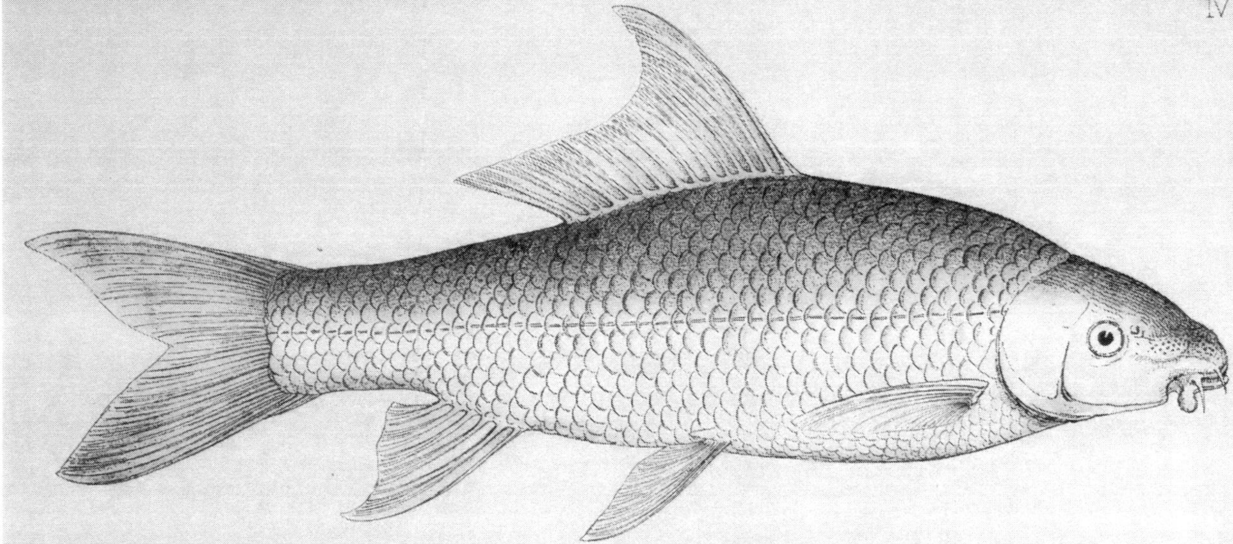

LABEO CALBASU.

London L. Reeve & Co

6. **Labeo cursa.**

HAB. Bengal. 3 feet.

CHAR. Scales along the lateral line 80. Lower lip finely fringed. Four minute barbels, the upper pair are sometimes absent.

7. **Labeo gonius.**

HAB. Bengal. 1½ feet.

CHAR. Scales 74. Lips fringed. Four small barbels.

8. **Labeo dussumieri.**

HAB. India and Ceylon. 1 foot.

CHAR. Scales 54. Lips fringed. Four minute barbels, of which the upper pair are sometimes absent.

Young examples have a large blackish spot on the end of the tail.

9 **Labeo rohita.** "The Roho."

HAB. India generally. Up to 3 feet.

This is perhaps the commonest of Indian fish, and the one most generally esteemed for eating purposes. It is to be found in all tanks and ponds, and, like other much domesticated fish, is often liable to variation. It grows to a large size. H. Buchanan remarks thus: "Of all fresh-water fish, so far as I have seen, it is perhaps the most excellent." The best are those taken in clear running water, and not too large.

It is deep in form, narrowing rather suddenly to the tail. Usually two barbels only, at the corners of the mouth, the rostral barbels being generally absent.

CHAR. Scales 41. Dorsal rays 16. Lips fringed.

10. **Labeo kontius.**

HAB. Madras. 2 feet.

CHAR. Scales 39. Dorsal rays 3+12.

Lower lip fringed, snout with lateral lobes. Eye behind the centre of the head.

11. **Labeo morala.**

HAB. Bengal.

This fish is only known from the figure and description given by Ham. Buchanan.

It has four barbels, lower lip indented on the edge, about 13 rays in the dorsal fin, and (according to the figure) about 32 scales along the lateral line. There is a black spot on the tail, and the darker colour of the back is extended down the side in very faint bars.

B. SPECIES WITHOUT ROSTRAL BARBELS.

The following three species are very similar to one another, they have 12 or 13 rays in the dorsal fin, 43 scales along the lateral line, five or six rows between the lateral line and the ventral fin.

They can best be recognised apart by the position of the eye.

12. **Labeo falcatus.**

HAB. Bengal and Assam. Attains 3 feet in length.

CHAR. The eye is situated far behind the centre of the head.

13. **Labeo ricnorhynchus.**

HAB. Base of the Himalayas, Bengal.

CHAR. The eye occupies the centre, or slightly behind the centre of the head. The lower lipis fringed.

14. Labeo diplostomus.

HAB. Cashmere and the Punjab.

CHAR. The eye is in advance of the centre of the head.

The following three species have a small lateral lobe to the snout, on each side. Lower lip not fringed. Eye behind the centre of the head.

15. Labeo bicolor.

HAB. N. W. Provinces and Assam.

CHAR. Scales 43. There are 7½ rows of scales between the lateral line and the ventral fin.

16. Labeo boga.

HAB. India generally, also Burmah.

CHAR. Scales 42. Five rows between the lateral line and the ventral fin.

17. Labeo pangusia.

HAB. Bengal and Cachar. 8 inches.

CHAR. Scales 40. Four and a half rows between the lateral line and the ventrals.

18. Labeo ariza.

HAB. India generally. 1 foot.

CHAR. Scales 37 to 40, transverse 15.

Eye in advance of the centre of the head. Lower lips slightly fringed. No lobes to the snout.

19. Labeo nukta.

HAB. Deccan. 1 foot.

CHAR. Scales 38, transverse 17.

Eye in the centre, or slightly behind the centre of the head. Lips not fringed.

COLOUR silvery, with some red marks on the scales.

20. **Labeo nashii.**

HAB. Base of the Coorg Hills. 4 inches.

CHAR. No barbels. Scales 41, transverse $13\frac{1}{2}$.

A black band from the eye to the centre of the caudal fin. A mark across the dorsal fin and the extremity of the caudal.

21. **Labæ striolatus.**

HAB. Deccan and Central Provinces. 7 inches.

CHAR. Scales 58 to 62. One pair of barbels.

GENUS CIRRHINA.

This genus contains some large and handsome fish, which are of considerable importance as food.

They are long in shape, elegantly formed, and of a brilliant golden, bronze, or silvery appearance, fully deserving the Sanscrit appellation of mirga (the deer), which has been appropriated as the scientific name of one species.

CHAR. The lips are thin and clean, neither of them being fringed; there is a small knob on the centre of the lower jaw, at the junction of the two mandibular bones, by which the fishes of this genus may generally be distinguished.

They have either one or two pairs of barbels, or none; when there is only one pair, they are on the snout, the pair at the corners of the mouth being absent. In this respect they differ from the Labeos.

1. Cirrhina mrigala.

HAB. Hindostan generally, attaining 18 lb. weight.

This is a fine fish, of elegant appearance, with bright golden scales, and very good for eating. I have never known of its being taken with a hook, but if suitable bait could be discovered I should think it would afford remarkably good sport.

Generally the rostral barbels only are present, the lower pair being rudimentary or absent.

It has from 40 to 43 scales along the lateral line, and 16 transversely. Dorsal fin rays 3+12 or 13.

CHAR. The origin of the dorsal fin is in advance of the central point between the end of the snout and the origin of the caudal fin, but not so far forward as in the next following species.

2. Cirrhina leschenaultii.

HAB. Southern and Central India. 1½ feet.

Very similar in appearance to *C. mrigala.*

Scales 42 to 44, transverse 17 or 18.

Dorsal rays 3+12 to 14. Barbels 4.

CHAR. Origin of the dorsal fin much nearer to the end of the snout than to the root of the caudal fin, it lies midway between the end of the snout and the hinder portion of the root of the anal fin.

3. Cirrhina anisura.

HAB. Bengal and Assam.

No barbels. Scales 43 or 44, transverse 18.

(M'Clelland in one part of his work states the scales as 38.)

CHAR. Dorsal rays 3+10. Lower lobe of caudal fin the longest. Dorsal fin commences midway between the end of the snout, and the root of the caudal.

4. **Cirrhina dyochilus.**

HAB. Clear running streams in Assam and Cachar.

"Its usual size is from one to two and a half feet in length, and though sometimes coarse, its flesh is always well flavoured."—*M'Clelland.*

No barbels. Scales 42 to 44, transverse 16.

CHAR. Dorsal rays 3+10. Dorsal commences in advance of the middle point between the end of the snout and the base of caudal fin.

5. **Cirrhina bata.**

HAB. Bengal. 1½ to 2 feet.

No barbels. Scales 36 to 39. Dorsal rays 2+9 or 10.

Lower lip smooth-edged. Caudal fin with an ill-defined transverse bar.

There is considerable uncertainty about this species, H. Buchanan described three varieties, which M'Clelland considered to belong to one species. Dr. Day's description differs in some respects from either of Buchanan's, but he states it to be a well-known fish, extensively used for stocking tanks. I have not met with it myself, and cannot therefore form any opinion of my own.

GENUS CROSSOCHILUS.

The species forming this genus are generally small, attaining five or six inches in length.

They have 10 or 11 rays in the dorsal fin, and 7 in the anal. From 35 to 40 scales along the lateral line, and 12 to 14 transverse rows.

CHAR. The mouth is placed underneath the snout, which projects more or less. The upper lip is fringed. Barbels four or two; if two, the upper only are present. The lower lip has a sharp inner edge, and is not continuous with the upper lip.

The fins are usually thick and fleshy, and the body is frequently irregularly marked with dark blotches.

1. Crossochilus latius.

HAB. Mountain streams of the Himalayas.

CHAR. Scales 39, $3\frac{1}{2}$ rows between the lateral line and the ventral fin. Barbels 4, of which the lower pair are sometimes absent.

Length of the head contained $5\frac{1}{2}$ times in the total. Eye somewhat behind the centre of the head.

2. Crossochilus gohama.

HAB. Bengal and Orissa. 6 inches.

CHAR. Scales 36; $3\frac{1}{2}$ rows between the lateral line and the ventral fin. Barbels 2. Head contained 5 times in the total.

Eye in, or slightly in advance of the centre of the head. Body irregularly spotted with brown.

3. **Crossochilus rostratus.**

HAB. Cossye River, Bengal.

CHAR. Scales 38; 4 rows between the lateral line and the ventral fin. Barbels 2. Snout long.

Head contained five times in the total length. Eye behind the centre of the head. An irregular black spot on the fifth and sixth scales of the lateral line.

4. **Crossochilus barbatulus.**

HAB. Cashmere and Punjab.

CHAR. Scales 36; 4 rows between lateral line and ventrals. Barbels 4. Head contained 5½ times in the total. Eye in the centre of the length of the head. Body more or less marked with dark blotches.

5. **Crossochilus sada.**

HAB. Assam.

CHAR. Barbels 4, longer than the diameter of the eye. Coloration uniform. This appears to be a very small species, but little is known about it.

6. **Crossochilus reba.**

HAB. India and Ceylon.

CHAR. Barbels 2. Scales 35 to 38; transverse 14, 4 or 5 rows between the lateral line and the ventral fin. Eye somewhat in advance of the middle of the head. Young individuals have the upper lips indistinctly fringed, old ones smooth.

(I have doubts about this fish being identical with

the *Gobio limnophilus* of M'Clelland, for the reason that this species has a pair of rostral barbels, which the latter has not. M'Clelland's fish is very abundant in the Sylhet district, where it forms a staple article of food, being taken in vast quantities, especially when the country begins to dry up, and the inundations to subside, about November. The fishermen build a screen of bamboo work at the mouth of a drainage cutting where the water that has flooded the fields for several months flows into a stream.

The fish trying to get back to the river are stopped by this impediment and crowd together in thousands, till the water boils with them. A second barrier is then built up a hundred yards or so above, and between these two screens the fish are kept, being bailed out by the fishermen as they are wanted, and sold at the weekly markets at the foot of the Khasia hills, both in a fresh and dried state.

In this part of the country this fish is called "Rhie." I am inclined to think, however, that it must be a distinct species from *Crossochilus reba*. If some person would forward a few specimens to the Calcutta museum, this point might be cleared up.)

7. Crossochilus mosario.

HAB. Assam. Length about a span.

CHAR. Barbels wanting.

Scales 37, transverse 12.

8. Crossochilus isurus.

HAB. River Hoogly.

CHAR. Barbels 2. Scales 36, transverse 10.

Origin of dorsal fin midway between the base of the last anal ray and the end of the snout.

Dr. Day identifies this fish with *Gobio isurus*, M'Cl., from Upper Assam. It does not, however, agree with M'Clelland's description.

GENUS DISCOGNATHUS.

These are small fishes living in rapid streams, among and under the stones. The lower lip is formed into a horny disk with free margins and is said to be used as a sucker for the purpose of clinging to the rocks. It certainly does assist it in holding on, but I should be inclined to doubt in this and other similar cases, the action of any suctorial power such as is possessed by the lamprey. One thing to be remembered is that in these rapid streams the rocks are invariably covered with a coating of slimy vegetable matter, on which these fishes seem to feed, but which would prevent any sucker apparatus from taking a hold of the stone, at least I should imagine so.

The pectoral and ventral fins are broad and thick and placed horizontally. By these arrangements these fish are able to cling firmly to the surface of the stones, even in a considerably strong current. Barbels 2 or 4. If 2, the upper pair are absent.

I was struck with an ingenious method of capturing these fish employed in the Central Provinces. The water was clear and shallow and numbers of these little fish could be seen, but it would have been a vain attempt to throw a net over them, as they would have escaped at once under and between the boulders. The fishermen therefore collected the boulders in heaps and left them thus for some days. Then, on coming to fish, they threw their casting-net over one of these heaps of stones, in which a lot of the fish had taken refuge. They then opened the centre of the net, and lifted the stones out one by one, till at last the fish alone were left in the net; in this way they secured a good number.

1. Discognathus lamta.

This fish is remarkable for the great extent of its geographical range. It is found from Palestine to Burmah, and has been described under many different names, as specimens from different localities are apt to differ slightly especially in the coloration. However, there is no specific distinction to be found between them.

There are about 34 scales along the lateral line and 9 transversely. There is a black spot behind the upper part of the gill opening.

CHAR. The pectoral fin is not longer than the head, and terminates at some distance from the root of the ventral fin.

2. Discognathus macrochir.

HAB. Bengal and Assam.

This species is very similar to *D. lamta*, and may possibly prove to be only a variety.

CHAR. Pectoral fin longer than the head, terminating close to the root of the ventral. Eye very small.

Chest and middle of abdomen scaleless; post pelvic region covered with very large scales.

This seems to agree pretty closely with the fish described by Dr. Day under the name of *Mayoa modesta.*

I have in my note-book a sketch of another species of *Discognathus* with 44 scales, from the base of the Khasia Hills. Dorsal rays 2+6.

GENUS PSILORHYNCHUS.

The two fishes belonging to this genus are found in the hill streams in N. E. Bengal and Assam. The snout is very long, the mouth underneath. Barbels none.

1. **Psilorhynchus sucatio.** 3 inches.

CHAR. Snout much longer than the rest of the head. Sides clouded with dots. Colour above greenish, below whitish and diaphanous, fins dotted.

2. **Psilorhynchus balitora.** 2 inches.

COLOUR reddish brown, with irregular black blotches, disposed in longitudinal rows. Three bars on the caudal fin. Body diaphanous.

GENUS OREINUS, "Mountain barbels."

These fishes are found in mountain streams, they have a silvery appearance, and are covered with very small scales. The dorsal fin has usually a very strong bony ray toothed interiorly. Dorsal rays 11. Anal 8. Barbels 4.

CHAR. Mouth transverse, on the lower surface of the snout. Margin of the lower jaw covered with a thick horny layer with a sharp edge. A broad fringed lower lip with a free posterior edge.

The anal fin and the vent. are contained in a sheath which is covered with enlarged tiled scales.

1. Oreinus plagiostomus.

HAB. Punjab, Cashmere, and Afghanistan.

Scales about 156, counting just above the lateral line; they are very irregular and difficult to count; on the lateral line itself they seem to run one into another, and thus appear larger than on the rest of the body; below, from the ventral fins forwards, they disappear altogether beneath the skin, which is thick and tough. These fish may be caught with worm or paste bait, and are eaten by the natives, but they are very bony and of a muddy flavour.

CHAR. Head contained about five times in the total length.

Margin of the lower lip straight.

Serrature of the dorsal fin rather feeble.

2. **Oreinus sinuatus.**

HAB. Himalayan rivers. Grows to 2 feet.

This fish has sometimes black dotted spots, and occasionally red spots, on which account it has been described as a Trout.

CHAR. Scales about 105.

Head contained $4\frac{1}{2}$ or 5 times in the total length.

Margin of lower lip concave.

Serrature of the dorsal fin well developed.

3. **Oreinus richardsonii.**

HAB. Nepal. Attains 18 inches.

CHAR. Head small, being contained $5\frac{1}{2}$ or 6 times in the total. Margin of lower lip straight.

Serrature of dorsal ray of moderate strength.

Scales 140 to 145.

4. **Oreinus micracanthus,** (*Capöeta*, Günth. Cat.)

HAB. Bhotan.

CHAR. Scales 140.

Head contained 5 or 6 times in the total length.

No bony dorsal ray.

GENUS SCHIZOTHORAX.

This genus differs from Oreinus in the form of the mouth, which is arched instead of being transverse.

They are found in Cashmere and Afghanistan, one or two species come from Nepal.

Most of the species of this genus are known only from the descriptions in Heckel's 'Fische aus Kaschmir,' and are difficult to distinguish. I can only indicate a few characteristics of each. Specimens are much wanted for the British Museum.

1. **Schizothorax planifrons.**

HAB. Cashmere. 14 inches.

CHAR. Osseous ray of dorsal fin coarsely serrated.

Head contained $3\frac{2}{3}$ times in the total length.

2. **Schizothorax micropogon.**

HAB. Cashmere. 6 inches.

CHAR. Mouth small, crescentic; barbels minute.

Dorsal ray coarsely serrated.

Head contained 4 times in the total.

3. **Schizothorax hugelii.**

HAB. Cashmere and Nepal. 16 inches.

CHAR. Dorsal ray rather short, and but slightly serrated.

Head contained $4\frac{1}{2}$ times in the total.

Anal scales very large.

Scales along the lateral line about 190.

4. **Schizothorax curvifrons.**

HAB. Cashmere.

CHAR. Dorsal ray conspicuously serrated.

Head contained $4\frac{1}{4}$ times in the total.

5. **Schizothorax niger.**

HAB. Cashmere. 7 inches.

CHAR. Dorsal ray with strong, closely-set teeth.

Sides with minute blackish dots.

Head contained $4\frac{1}{2}$ times in the total.

6. **Schizothorax nasus.**

HAB. Cashmere. 11 inches.

CHAR. Dorsal with teeth not very closely set.

Head contained 4½ times in the total.

7. **Schizothorax longipinnis.**

HAB. Cashmere. 10 inches.

CHAR. Dorsal ray with closely set teeth.

Head contained 4½ times in the total.

8. **Schizothorax esocinus.**

HAB. Cashmere and Afghanistan. 10 inches.

CHAR. Head depressed, much elongate, with long snout, contained 3½ times in the total.

Dorsal ray with strong closely set teeth.

Body with numerous blackish dots.

9. **Schizothorax gobioides.**

HAB. Nepal. 8½ inches.

CHAR. Dorsal ray moderately strong.

Barbels long, their length being greater than the diameter of the eye. Anal scales very slightly enlarged.

COLOUR yellowish, with minute black spots.

10. **Schizothorax nobilis.**

HAB. Nepal and Afghanistan. 18 inches.

CHAR. Dorsal spine strong, with rather feeble serrature. Length of rostral barbels 1½ diameters of the eye. Maxillary pair nearly as long. Caudal fin deeply forked. Anal scales moderately developed.

COLOUR silvery, covered with small spots.

11. Schizothorax hodgsonii.

Hab. Himalayan streams. 20 inches.

Char. Lower labial fold broad, with a free edge; it is not interrupted in the middle like that of all the foregoing species, but is produced in a small lobe or projection. Snout long and pointed. Head contained 4 times in the total length. Dorsal ray with very strong teeth.

GENUS CAPÖETA.

This genus is distributed over Western and Southern Asia. Two species are to be found in the hill streams of Sinde and those of the Punjab that flow into the river Indus.

Char. Mouth transverse, inferior, with the edge of the lower jaw nearly straight and sharp, the corners bent angularly inwards.

1. Capöeta watsoni.

Char. Scales 33, transverse 6+6.

Barbels. One pair at the corners of the mouth.

Dorsal ray strong and serrated.

Colour silvery, dashed with gold. Various and very irregular black spots on the body.

2. Capöeta irregularis.

Char. Scales 36, transverse 9+9. Scales above the lateral line very irregularly disposed.

Dorsal ray weak and serrated.

Colour olive, shot with gold.

GENUS CATLA.

This genus is represented by a single species.

Char. The junction of the two bones forming the lower jaw is loose, without any knob. The snout is broad, and the mouth turned upwards. There is no upper lip.

1. **Catla buchanani.**

Hab. Upper India, ponds and rivers, attaining a very large size. This fish may be at once recognised by its very large head, and the peculiar upturned mouth. It is well adapted for stocking tanks, as it grows quickly and is good and wholesome as food.

Char. Scales 40 to 43. Dorsal rays 2+16.
Length of head contained 3 times in the total.

The foregoing species are all included in the group *Cyprinina*, or Carp-like fishes, of the family *Cyprinidæ*.

We come next to the group Rasborina.

GENUS RASBORA.

These are handsome little fishes, brightly coloured, and generally with a dark band running the whole length of the body.

Geographical Distribution. Species of this genus are found in the East Indian Continent and Archipelago, also on the East Coast of Africa.

Char. The lateral line curves downwards and runs along the lower half of the body and tail. Barbels wanting, except in Rasbora elanga, which has a small pair.

V

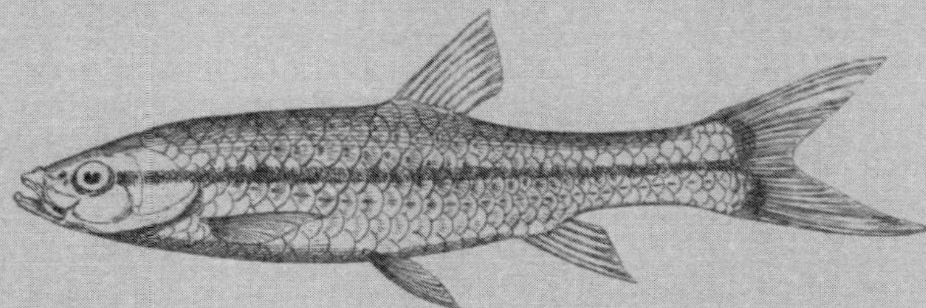

RASBORA DANICORNIUS.

London: L. Reeve & Co.

1. Rasbora daniconius.

This is a very common little fish, being found in every tank and pond. It is brilliantly coloured when living with purple and green irradiations, and has a black band running the whole length of the body, from the eye to the end of the tail.

It grows to about 5 inches in length. It is very active and voracious, and will rise readily to a fly, or go at a bit of worm on a hook, but the very smallest hooks, and the finest tackle are required to secure it.

CHAR. Scales 31 or 32. A black band runs the whole length of the body. Sometimes the caudal fin is tipped with black.

2. Rasbora buchanani.

HAB. Bengal and Assam. 4 or 5 inches.

CHAR. Scales 25 to 29.

A faint silvery streak along the side, colour usually yellow, with black tips to the caudal fin.

3. Rasbora neilgherriensis.

HAB. Madras. 8 inches.

CHAR. Scales 34.

A silvery leaden band from the eye to the base of the caudal fin.

4. Rasbora elanga.

HAB. Bengal and Assam. 8 inches.

CHAR. Scales 40.

A pair of very small barbels near the upper end of the maxillaries. Colour uniform silvery.

GENUS NURIA.

CHAR. Barbels 4, the upper pair being short, and the pair at the corners of the mouth long.

Mouth narrow, directed obliquely upwards.

1. **Nuria danrica.**

HAB. India generally. 4 inches.

This is a handsome little fish, with a black band running the whole length of the body, from the end of the snout, through the eye, to the base of the caudal fin.

This species does well in an aquarium, and it is interesting to watch its habits. Each fish selects its own bit of water, and remains swimming up and down in it, keeping off all intruders. It feeds principally on water weeds, for nibbling at which its upturned mouth seems admirably adapted. It has also a habit of floating at the surface, which the mouth just touches, the two upper cirri are then extended forwards, and seem to guide towards the fish's mouth any minute insects that may happen to be floating within the influence of the current which is established by the breathing of the fish.

These fish are sometimes found in hot springs.

CHAR. Scales 29 to 31. Lateral line complete.

2. **Nuria malabarica.**

HAB. Southern India. 3 inches.

CHAR. Scales 32. Lateral line absent.

GENUS AMBLYPHARYNGODON.

CHAR. Small fishes, not exceeding 4 inches in length. Barbels none. Lateral line incomplete. Mouth directed somewhat upwards, with the lower jaw prominent. Scales very small.

COLOUR silvery, with a bright silvery band along the middle of the side.

1. **Amblypharyngodon mola.**

HAB. India generally.

CHAR. Scales 65. Height of body contained 3 times, length of head $3\frac{1}{2}$ times, in the total length.

Anterior ray of the dorsal fin directly above the posterior ray of the ventral.

2. **Amblypharyngodon pellucidus.**

HAB. Bengal and Assam.

CHAR. Scales 55. Height of body contained 4 times, length of head $3\frac{1}{3}$ times, in the total length.

Anterior ray of the dorsal fin directly above the posterior ray of the ventral.

3. **Amblypharyngodon melettinus.**

HAB. Southern and Western India.

CHAR. Scales 50 to 57. Height of body contained 4 times, head 4 times, in the total length.

Origin of the dorsal fin entirely behind the root of the ventral.

GENUS THYNNICHTHYS.

CHAR. Lateral line complete. Barbels none.

Very similar to *Amblypharyngodon*, but attains a larger size.

1. **Thynnichthys harengula.**

HAB. Godavery and Kistna rivers. 1 foot.

It also breeds in tanks.

CHAR. Scales 120. Dorsal fin commences above the ventrals, and slightly nearer to the snout than to the base of the caudal fin.

The next group are the *Semiplotina*, of which there are only two Indian species known.

GENUS SEMIPLOTUS.

CHAR. No barbels. Lateral line runs along the middle of the side of the tail. Anal fin short, not extending forwards to below the dorsal. Dorsal fin long, with a strong osseous ray. Mouth large, semicircular, inferior.

1. **Semiplotus M'Clellandi.**

HAB. Assam. Up to 2½ lb. weight, 12 to 20 inches long.

"It is usually found near rapids; the larger ones in deeper waters, where they are seen, particularly of an evening, rising to the surface, but they refuse all sorts of flies and baits, although if a stone be cast into the water, all these fishes in the vicinity assemble round the spot. The dhoms (fishermen) take them by a casting net, observing great silence, and frequently first dropping a stone to assemble the fish in the spot on which it is intended to cast the net."—*Griffith.*

"This species which is considered the most delicious in Assam, is found only in the upper parts of the province, where the currents become clear and somewhat rapid. It is common at Suddyah, and is said to be found from thence to the foot of the mountains."

"Head covered with a thick skin."—*M'Clelland.*

CHAR. Scales 30 to 32. Dorsal fin with a strong, smooth ray, and about 25 branched rays. Anal rays 9.

2. Semiplotus brevidorsalis.

HAB. Rivers of the Neilgherry Hills.

CHAR. Scales 40. Dorsal rays 14. Anal 7.

The following group, *Danionina*, contains a variety of bright coloured little fishes, none of which attain a large size.

CHAR. Anal fin with 8, or more than 8, branched rays. The lateral line runs along the lower half of the tail. Abdomen rounded (not compressed into a sharp ridge).

GENUS DANIO.

CHAR. Dorsal fin long (with nine, or more, branched rays), mouth directed obliquely upwards, narrow. Barbels generally four, sometimes two only, or none.

1. **Danio dangilia.**

HAB. Bengal and Behar. 5 or 6 inches.

CHAR. Dorsal rays 2+10. Anal 17 to 20. Scales 36 to 38. Barbels four, the upper pair being rather shorter than the head, the lower pair longer than the head.

Sides with a network of narrow blue lines, anal fin with two or three blue stripes.

2. **Danio lineolatus.**

HAB. Sikkim. 3 inches.

CHAR. Dorsal rays 13 or 14. Anal 16 or 17. Scales 32 or 33.

Barbels four, the upper pair as long as the diameter of the eye, the lower pair very short.

Sides with three straight, bluish bands, the middle one being the broadest, alternated with yellow.

3. **Danio osteographus,** (*micronema*, Günther).

HAB. India generally. 6 inches.

CHAR. Dorsal 12 or 14. Anal 15 to 17. Scales 34 to 37.

Barbels four, the upper pair half as long as the orbit, the lower pair minute or absent.

Sides with straight bluish bands, the centre one being the broadest, and being continued down the caudal fin.

4. **Danio aurolineatus,** (*malabaricus*, Günth).

HAB. South Malabar. 3 inches.

CHAR. Dorsal 14. Anal 18. Scales 34 to 40.

Barbels two only, half as long as the eye.

Sides with three or four narrow steel blue streaks, the end of the tail, and the middle of the caudal fin with a broad bluish band.

5. **Danio neilgherriensis.**

HAB. Neilgherry Hills. 3½ inches.

CHAR. Dorsal 12 or 13. Anal 13 or 14. Scales 35.

Barbels 2 only, very small, sometimes a rudimentary lower pair are apparent. A badly marked, broad, steel-blue stripe, extending from behind the eye to the middle of the caudal fin, edged with yellow above and below.

A species very similar to this last one is common in the hill streams at Cherra-poonjee in the Khasia Hills. I should not be surprised if it turned out identical with M'Clelland's *Perilampus æquipinnatus.* The fish which Dr. Day has identified under this name appears to differ from M'Clelland's in possessing a well developed rostral pair of barbels, which M'Clelland does not mention, neither are they shown in the figure. The species I refer to from the Khasia Hills has no barbels, or if present they must be excessively minute. It has several blue and yellow streaks along the sides.

6. **Danio devario.**

HAB. Northern India, Assam. 4 inches.

CHAR. The fin rays appear to vary considerably, the average numbers seem to be Dorsal 18. Anal 18.

Scales 40 or 41. Barbels none. Head small.

Body deep, marked with blue lines, forming a network towards the head, and longitudinal stripes near the tail, one stripe is continued along the tail; and the upper portion of the caudal fin.

GENUS PTEROPSARION.*

CHAR. Dorsal fin long, with nine, or more, branched rays, mouth wide, directed obliquely upwards. Barbels none.

1. **Pteropsarion bakeri.**

HAB. Hill ranges of Travancore. 6 inches.

CHAR. Dorsal rays 13. Anal 16 or 17. Scales 38.

A row of large bluish spots along the sides of the body. Dark grey marks on all the fins. No barbels.

* Dr. Day classes this fish as a *Barilius*, from which genus it is excluded by Dr. Günther, apparently on account of its long dorsal fin. As the point is one perfectly immaterial to the student, I prefer to follow the standard authority.

GENUS BARILIUS.

GEOGRAPHICAL DISTRIBUTION. This genus is found on the Continent of India and the East of Africa, including the River Nile.

CHAR. Dorsal fin short (less than 9 soft rays). Mouth wide, opening forwards, Barbels 4, or 2, or none.

We can divide the species, for convenience, into three groups, according to the number, or want, of barbels. It is not however a natural division, as frequently the barbels are so small as to be hardly perceptible—or wanting, in species that would normally possess them.

Where not otherwise mentioned, the rays of the dorsal fin, are 9 or 10, those of the anal fin about 12, and the number of scales along the body about 43.

A. SPECIES WITH FOUR BARBELS.

1. Barilius rerio.

This is one of the smallest of Indian fishes, it is easily recognised by the indigo-blue bands running the whole length of the body, extending over the caudal and anal fins.

HAB. Bengal and Madras. Attaining 2 inches.

CHAR. Dorsal rays 9. Anal 15. Scales 27.

Two pairs of small barbels.

2. Barilius radiolatus.

HAB. Central India. $2\frac{1}{2}$ inches.

CHAR. Scales 56 to 58. Two pairs of short barbels.

3. **Barilius alburnus.**

HAB. Himalayan streams. 5 inches.

CHAR. Anal rays 13 or 14.

Depth of body contained $5\frac{1}{2}$ times, length of head $4\frac{1}{2}$ to 5 times, in the total length. The two last rays of the dorsal fin arise over the root of the anal. The humeral process, (a bony projection just above the pectoral fin) is very short. Ten or twelve blackish bars descend from the back to the lateral line.

4. **Barilius bendelesis.**

HAB. River Ganges and Southern India. $4\frac{1}{2}$ inches.

CHAR. Depth of body contained 4 times, head $4\frac{1}{4}$, in the total. Dorsal fin terminates in advance of the anal.

A series of short, green or bluish, bars on the side not reaching the lateral-line. Some of the scales have occasionally a black spot at their bases.

5. **Barilius cocsa.**

HAB. India generally. 6 inches.

CHAR. Anal rays 10. Depth of body contained 4 times, head $4\frac{1}{2}$ times, in the total. Barbels 4, minute, the upper pair being often absent. Dorsal fin terminates in advance of the anal. Humeral process elongate.

The back, in young specimens, with indistinct crossbars. Each scale with a small black spot at the base, a row of double spots forming the lateral line.

6. **Barilius modestus.**

HAB. Lahore river Ravi. 4 inches.

CHAR. Depth $3\frac{3}{4}$ times, head $4\frac{1}{2}$ times, in the total length.

Barbels 4, the lower pair minute.

The last ray of the dorsal fin over the first ray of the anal.

Humeral process short. No bars or bands. Caudal fin edged with black.

7. **Barilius bleekeri.**

HAB. River Beeas, Punjab. 3 inches.

CHAR. Depth 4 times, head 4 times, in the total.

Barbels 4, long, reaching to below the eye. The one or two last rays of the dorsal fin over the first of the anal. Seven short bluish bars down the middle of the side.

Caudal fin stained on the outer edge.

B. SPECIES WITH ONE PAIR OF BARBELS.

8. **Barilius morarensis.**

HAB. River Omorar, Gwalior. 3 inches.

CHAR. Barbels 2, very small. Depth $4\frac{1}{3}$ times, head $4\frac{1}{2}$ times, in the total. Dorsal fin altogether in advance of the anal.

Humeral process very short. Crossbars indistinct.

9. **Barilius bicirratus.**

HAB. Cabul River.

CHAR. Scales 35. Nine incomplete bars down the sides.

10. **Barilius barila.**

HAB. Bengal. 4 inches.

CHAR. Barbels two, small, sometimes wanting.

Depth $4\frac{1}{2}$ times, head $4\frac{1}{2}$ times, in total. The last ray of the dorsal fin is opposite the first ray of the anal.

About 14 blue bars down the middle of the side.

Buchanan mentions that there are two lateral lines, the upper one being straight, and the lower one curved. The latter is the true lateral line.

11. **Barilius vagra.**

HAB. Bengal and N.W. Provinces. 5 inches.

CHAR. Scales 42 to 45. Two short barbels.

Depth contained 3 times, head $3\frac{3}{4}$ times, in the total.

COLOUR silvery, with a light coloured stripe and indistinct crossbars.

C. SPECIES WANTING BARBELS.

12. **Barilius barna.**

HAB. Bengal Assam, and N.W. Provinces. 4 inches,

CHAR. Barbels none. Depth contained 3, head 4 times, in the total. The last three rays of the dorsal fin are opposite to the anal. About nine bluish black bars across the body. Dorsal and caudal fins tipped with black. In this species also Buchanan mentions an upper, straight, lateral line.

13. **Barilius gatensis.**

HAB. Western Ghats and Neilgherry hills. 6 inches.

CHAR. Barbels none. Dorsal rays 10. Anal 16. Scales 38 to 40.

Depth contained $3\frac{1}{3}$, head $3\frac{3}{4}$ times, in the total. Last four rays of the dorsal fin opposite the anal. About 15 irregular bluish bars. Dorsal and anal fins with dark bases and light margins.

14. **Barilius papillatus.**

HAB. Bengal. 3 inches.

CHAR. Barbels none. Dorsal rays 10. Anal 14. Scales 39.

Depth contained 3 times, head 4 times, in the total.

About 8 broad, deep blue, bars right across the body.

15. **Barilius borelio.**

HAB. Bengal. 4 inches.

CHAR. Barbels none. Scales 39.

Depth contained 4 times, head 4 times, in the total.

COLOUR silvery, tinged with green, fins yellowish, dorsal fin edged with grey. No crossbars.

16. **Barilius canarensis.**

HAB. Western Coast. 6 inches.

CHAR. Barbels none. Dorsal rays 12. Anal, 15. Scales 38.

Depth contained 3 times, head $3\frac{1}{2}$ times, in the total.

A double row of large green spots along the body, joining on the tail into a single row.

Fins grey with broad white margins.

17. **Barilius tileo.**

HAB. Bengal and Assam. 8 inches.

CHAR. Barbels none. Dorsal rays 10. Anal 14. Scales 66 to 70.

Two rows of greenish blue spots along the side.

18. **Barilius evezardi.**

HAB. Poona, Bombay. $4\frac{1}{2}$ inches.

CHAR. Barbels none. Dorsal rays 9. Anal 15. Scales 40.

The lower lobe of the caudal fin is the longest.

Fins deep orange, dorsal and caudal edged with black.

Depth contained $3\frac{2}{3}$ times, head $4\frac{1}{2}$ times, in the total.

COLOUR silvery, without bars.

GENUS BOLA.

There is only one known species belonging to this genus.

CHAR. Scales small, mouth very wide and deeply cleft. Barbels none. Dorsal fin short.

1. **Bola Goha.**

This is a finely formed fish, and with its small scales, numerous spots, and large mouth, reminds one strongly of a Trout. The resemblance, however, is only a superficial one, as the family Salmonidæ are to be distinguished at once by the second, or adipose dorsal fin, and have no representatives in the Indian waters.

HAB. Northern India. Grows to a foot in length.

CHAR. Dorsal rays 10. Anal 12. Scales about 90.

COLOUR silvery, with several irregular series of greenish spots along the side.

Fins orange; caudal edged with black.

GENUS SCHACRA.

This genus also contains only one species.

CHAR. Mouth of moderate width, opening forwards; the upper jaw projecting slightly. Scales small.

Barbels four. Dorsal fin short.

1. Schacra cirrhata.

HAB. Bengal, Assam, and N. W. Provinces. 4 or 5 inches.

CHAR. Scales 72. Dorsal rays 9. Anal 10.

COLOUR silvery, with about 13 bluish, incomplete bars, down the middle of the side. Caudal fin stained with black on the lower half. Barbels 4.

GENUS ASPIDOPARIA.

CHAR. Mouth narrow, crescent shaped, situated below the snout. Dorsal fin short. Barbels none.

1 Aspidoparia morar.

HAB. Northern India. 6 inches.

CHAR. Dorsal rays 10. Anal 11. Scales 38 to 42.

Head contained $3\frac{1}{2}$ times in the total length. Height of body 4 times nearly. Pectoral fin shorter than the head.

2. Aspidoparia sardina.

HAB. Northern India. 4 inches.

Dr. Day considers this identical with the preceding species.

The following are the apparent points of difference.

CHAR. Head contained $4\frac{1}{2}$ times in the total. Scales 37.

Pectoral fin at least as long as the head.

3. **Aspidoparia jaya.**

HAB. Gangetic provinces. 2 inches.

CHAR. Scales 54 to 58.

The next group we have to notice are the *Abramidina.*

They have a long anal fin. The abdomen, or a portion of it, is sometimes compressed into a sharp ridge, in a manner similar to what occurs in the family Clupeidæ or Herrings. Barbels none.

GENUS OSTEOBRAMA.

CHAR. Pectoral fins of moderate length. A strong serrated spine to the dorsal fin. Scales small. Lateral line running nearly in the middle of the tail. Dorsal rays 11. The different species may most readily be distinguished by the number of rays in the anal fin, and the number of the scales.

GEOGRAPHICAL DISTRIBUTION. India and Burmah.

1. **Osteobrama cotio.**

HAB. India generally. 4 inches.

CHAR. Anal rays 29 to 32. Scales 70. Barbels none. Depth of body contained $2\frac{2}{3}$ times, head $4\frac{1}{5}$ times, in the total. Dorsal ray not very strong. Jaws even in front. Scales below the lateral line rather irregular.

2. **Osteobrama alfrediana.**

Hab. Bengal and Assam. 6 inches.

Char. Anal rays 31 to 36. Scales 42 to 60. Barbels none.

Depth contained $2\frac{1}{2}$ times, head $4\frac{1}{3}$ times, in the total. Dorsal ray slender, and but slightly serrated. Upper jaw projecting slightly over the lower. Lateral line very strongly marked in the first few scales.

If these two species be really distinct, it seems to me that this latter must be the one described by Ham. Buchanan as Cyprinus cotio. He distinctly states the rays of the anal fin as 36, and according to the figure the scales would be between 40 and 50.

If, however, as noted by Dr. Day, the native name of the first species is, "Koti," and of the second, "Goonta," and they are really distinct; then, even if my surmise be correct, it will probably be more convenient to leave the names as they stand. Buchanan can hardly be said to have named the fish he described, but simply to have misappropriated the native name of a nearly allied species.

3. **Osteobrama rapax.**

Hab. Northern India. 8 inches.

Char. Anal rays 25 or 26. Scales 75. Barbels none.

Depth contained 3 times, head $3\frac{4}{5}$ times, in the total. Dorsal ray strong, and deeply denticulated.

Lower jaw slightly projecting. Lateral line most strongly developed in the first few scales.

4. Osteobrama ogilbii.

HAB. India generally.

CHAR. Anal rays 15 or 16. Scales 50 to 55. Barbels none.

Depth contained $2\frac{1}{4}$ times, head 4 times, in the total.

Dorsal ray deeply serrated. The upper jaw projects in advance of the lower. Lateral line slightly bent downwards.

An indistinct blotch on the root of the caudal fin.

5. Osteobrama microlepis.

HAB. River Godavery. 15 inches.

CHAR. Anal rays 21. Scales 72. Barbels none.

Depth contained $2\frac{1}{4}$ times, head 4 times, in the total. Dorsal ray strong and serrated.

Upper jaw projects beyond the lower. A dark streak from the shoulder to the pectoral fin. Body partially banded, especially in the young.

Dr. Day suggests that the fish described by Valenciennes as Lennsius belangeri, and in the British Museum Catalogue as Similiogaster belangerii, may be this species. Should this be the fact, the name of the fish would, I conclude, be properly Osteobrama belangerii, and not microlepis.

6. Osteobrama neilli.

HAB. Rivers of the Neilgherries.

CHAR. Barbels four, nearly as long as the eye. Anal rays 21. Scales 59.

Depth contained $2\frac{2}{3}$ times, head $3\frac{1}{3}$ times, in the total.

Lateral line strongly marked in the first few scales. Scales regular.

7. **Osteobrama bakeri.**

HAB. Cottyam. $4\frac{1}{2}$ inches.

CHAR. Anal rays 14. Scales 44. Barbels four, short.

Depth contained $3\frac{1}{4}$ times, head 4 times, in the total.

COLOUR silvery, caudal and dorsal fins edged with black.

GENUS CHELA.

These are bright silvery fishes, termed Chilwas in Hindostani, they are long in the body, with small heads and upturned mouths, the dorsal fin being placed very far back.

They keep mostly at the surface of the water, feeding on insects, and may be taken with the artificial fly.

They are remarkably good eating when fried.

GEOGRAPHICAL DISTRIBUTION. This genus is distributed over the continent of India, Burmah, and the East Indian Archipelago.

CHAR. Pectoral fins very long, no spine to the dorsal fin. Not less than 7 rays in the ventral fin.

Abdomen compressed, forming a sharp ridge.

The dorsal fin contains 9 or 10 rays, the anal varies in length.

1. **Chela gora.**

HAB. Northern India. 8 inches.

CHAR. Anal rays 15. Scales 140 to 160.

The scales of the back extend over the nape as far as the nostrils. The ring of small bony plates, situated behind and below the eye, is broad, but does not entirely cover the foremost gill plate, or præoperculum.

The abdomen, in front of the ventral fins, is rounded, further back it has a sharp edge.

The dorsal fin commences slightly in advance of the anal.

2. **Chela bacaila.**

HAB. Throughout India. 6 inches.

CHAR. Anal rays 14 to 16. Scales 90 to 110.

Nuchal scales extend forwards not so far as the eye. Suborbital ring broad, nearly covering the præoperculum. Origin of the first anal ray below the middle of the dorsal fin.

3. **Chela punjabensis.**

HAB. Ravi River, at Lahore.

CHAR. Anal rays 17. Scales about 110.

Nuchal scales extend forwards to opposite the suborbital ring of bones. Suborbital ring broad, covering three-fourths of the cheek. Abdominal edge sharp, from the pectorals backwards.

Silvery, with a burnished silvery band along the side.

4. **Chela phulo.**

HAB. Bengal and Central India. 4 inches.

CHAR. Anal 20. Scales 87.

Suborbital bones cover two-thirds of the cheek.

Dorsal fin commences slightly behind the origin of the anal. Abdominal edge sharp from the pectorals backwards.

Silvery, with a burnished band along the side.

5. **Chela clupeoides.**

HAB. Madras, Mysore, and the Dekkan. 6 inches.

CHAR. Anal rays 14. Scales 80.

Suborbital ring narrower than the diameter of the eye.

Origin of the dorsal fin very slightly in advance of the anal. Thorax compressed into a cutting edge.

Scales loosely attached, and placed in irregular rows.

6. **Chela flavipinnis.**

HAB. Madras Presidency.

CHAR. Anal rays 18. Scales 65.

Suborbital ring nearly covering the cheek. Five small indentations on the edge of the prœopercular plate.

COLOUR silvery, fins tipped with orange.

7. **Chela novacula.**

HAB. India.

CHAR. Anal rays 17. Scales 60.

The height of the body is more than the length of the head.

8. **Chela untrahi.**

HAB. Mahanadi River. 5 inches.

CHAR. Anal rays 20. Scales 52.

Abdomen sharp from the pectorals backwards.

Lower jaw prominent.

Scales deciduous, extending forwards on the nape to above the posterior margin of the orbit.

Pectoral fin, when laid backwards, reaches the ventral.

9. **Chela argentea.**

HAB. Bowany River, at the base of the Neilgherries. 6 inches.

This species is perhaps the same as the Chela diffusa which comes from the Cauvery River, in which case the latter name would have to be adopted, as having the priority.

CHAR. Anal rays 18. Scales 43 to 45.

Suborbital ring broad, covering the cheek.

Lower jaw not projecting. Origin of anal below the foremost rays of the dorsal fin.

Pectoral fin very long, extending beyond the origin of the ventral. Thorax not sharp.

10. **Chela boopis.**

HAB. South Canara. 5 inches.

CHAR. Anal rays 18. Scales 37.

Suborbital ring broad, nearly covering the cheek. Origin of anal below the hinder part of the dorsal fin.

Eyes large. Thorax smooth. Dorsal, anal, and caudal fins tipped with black.

The two following species differ from all the species previously described in not being so long in the body.

By Drs. M'Clelland and Day they are placed in a distinct genus,—Perilampus.

11. **Chela laubuca.**

Hab. Bengal. 3 inches.

Char. Anal rays 22 to 24. Scales 34 to 37.

Body deep, its height being contained barely 3 times in the total length. The scales of the back do not extend in front of the edge of the operculum, or gill cover.

Pectoral fin very long, reaching the anal.

Origin of the dorsal fin behind the origin of the anal.

A black mark, shot with green, at the base of the pectoral, and one at the base of the caudal fin.

12. **Chela perseus.**

Hab. Assam. 3 inches.

Char. Anal rays 21.

Depth of body contained 3 times in the total length.

Mouth opens upwards. Scales of the nape extend to the margin of the prœoperculum. Back straight from the mouth to the dorsal fin.

A blue streak along the side.

GENUS CACHIUS.

Char. Pectoral fins very long. No spine to the dorsal fin. Less than seven rays in the ventral fins, which are placed far forwards, nearly beneath the pectorals, one ray of each ventral fin being produced into a long filament.

1. **Cachius atpar.**

Hab. India generally. 4 inches.

Char. Anal rays 22 to 26. Scales 52 to 55.

Dorsal fin opposite the middle of the anal. The first ray of the ventral prolonged into a long bristle, the other rays being quite rudimental.

Colour greenish, with a silvery lateral band.

The next group, Homalopterina, contains only one genus, which differs from the members of the other groups in not possessing an air bladder.

It appears to be confined to India, Burmah, and the Islands of Java and Sumatra.

GENUS HOMALOPTERA.

Char. Dorsal and anal fins short, the former opposite to the ventrals. Pectoral and ventral fins placed horizontally. Barbels six, 4 on the snout, and two at the corners of the mouth.

1. **Homaloptera maculata.**

Hab. Hill streams of the N. Eastern Frontier.

Char. Scales 78. No scales on the thorax.

Snout very broad and depressed, with sharp margins.

Barbels very small, the two rostral pairs beneath the end of the snout.

Colour dark brown, with darker blotches.

2. **Homaloptera brucei.**

Hab. Southern India. $3\frac{1}{2}$ inches.

Char. Scales 70?

Snout broad and depressed, with the margin obtuse.

Rostral barbels short, on the edge of the snout; the pair at the corners of the mouth rather bigger.

Colour dull olive, yellowish below. Body with large brown blotches.

The next, and last, group of the family Cyprinidæ, are the Cobitidina, or Loaches.

They might almost deserve to be ranked as a separate family, but the line of demarcation is so faintly defined, that they have been included in the family of the Cyprinidæ. The most distinctive peculiarity among them lies in the air-bladder, which is partially, or entirely, enclosed in a bony capsule.

They live altogether at the bottom of the water, and many of them bury themselves in sand or mud. They are generally small, and of no great importance, or interest, although the species inhabiting Indian fresh waters are numerous.

It will suffice therefore to give a list of the various species as yet known, without entering into any detailed descripton.

Char. Mouth surrounded by six, or more, barbels. Anal fin short. Scales small, or rudimentary, or wanting altogether.

GENUS MISGURNUS.

CHAR. Barbels ten or twelve. Caudal fin rounded.

1. **Misgurnus lateralis.**

HAB. Bengal. $3\frac{1}{2}$ inches.

CHAR. Barbels 10. Scales very conspicuous.

Yellow and brown bands along the side. A black white-edged ocellus on the base of the upper half of the caudal fin.

GENUS NEMACHILUS.

CHAR. Barbels six (or eight).

No erectile spine under the eye.

1. **Nemachilus pavonaceous.**

HAB. Assam. Dorsal rays 17. About 20 bars across the back.

An eye-like spot on the upper part of the end of the tail.

2. **Nemachilus botia.**

HAB. Throughout India. Dorsal rays 14.

CHAR. Body with irregular black blotches, caudal fin barred.

3. **Nemachilus rupelli.**

HAB. Poona. Dorsal rays 12 or 13.

Short brown bars along the lateral line. Fin rays barred. A black spot at the base of the upper lobe of the caudal fin.

4. **Nemachilus moreh.**

HAB. Poona. Dorsal rays 12. Caudal wedge-shaped, very similar to rupelli, but with the head more pointed.

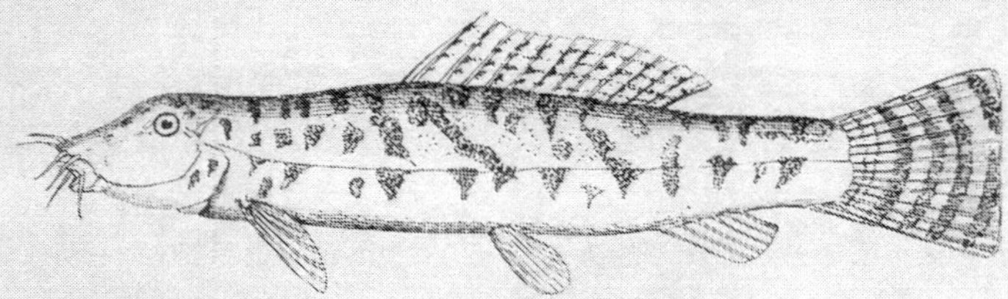

NEMACHILUS BOTIA.

London: L. Reeve & Co.

5. **Nemachilus monoceros.**

HAB. Assam. Dorsal rays 12. Dorsal and caudal fins with transverse stripes. Body without markings.

6. **Nemachilus aureus.**

HAB. Nerbudda River. Dorsal rays 12.

COLOUR greenish, with, in the young, a row of seven or eight blotches along the side. Caudal barred, with a dark ocellus.

7. **Nemachilus rupecola.**

HAB. Northern India. Dorsal rays 10 or 11. Caudal fin with rounded lobes. 11 to 17 dark cross-bands; a black spot at the base of the dorsal fin. Fins spotted.

8. **Nemachilus semiarmatus.**

HAB. Neilgherry Hills. Dorsal rays 11.

Marked irregularly with dark spots and bars.

Pectoral fin with a partially osseous ray.

The remaining species have all about 10 rays in the dorsal fin. Some of them are banded, and others irregularly marked.

9. **Nemachilus montanus.**

HAB. Near Simla. 12 brown bands. Caudal fin forked.

10. **Nemachilus beavani.**

HAB. Bengal. 9 dark bands. Caudal fin slightly forked.

11. **Nemachilus subfuscus.**

Hab. Assam.

10 narrow brown bands. Caudal forked.

12. **Nemachilus denisonii.**

Hab. Neilgherries.

9 to 12 dark bands. Caudal forked.

13. **Nemachilus notostigma.**

Hab. Cauvery River.

12 or 13 brown bands. A black streak across the root of the caudal. A black spot at the base of the anterior dorsal rays.

14. **Nemachilus triangularis.**

Hab. Travancore Hills.

Body with about eight dark, blackedged bands, they are bent in the middle, the angles pointing backwards. A black spot at the root of, and three black bars across the caudal fin.

15. **Nemachilus striatus.**

Hab. Wynaad Hills.

Light reddish brown with narrow vertical bands, fins orange with black markings.

16. **Nemachilus zonatus.**

Hab. Northern India.

11 to 13 dark zones, not meeting under the body.

17. **Nemachilus sinuatus.**

Hab. Wynaad.

Orange with four bent bands.

18. **Nemachilus mugah.**

HAB. Bengal.

About 15 brown bands, descending below the lateral line.

19. **Nemachilus rubripinnis.**

HAB. Malabar.

Nine bands, not reaching the lateral line, also a number of irregular bars.

20. **Nemachilus savona.**

HAB. Bengal.

Ten or twelve very narrow yellow or white bands; a black blotch at the base of the first few rays of the dorsal fin.

The remaining species are not banded down the sides.

21. **Nemachilus marmoratus.**

HAB. Cashmere.

Body mottled with brown.

Margin of caudal fin convex.

22. **Nemachilus spilopterus.**

HAB. Himalayan streams.

11 to 15 irregular bars across the back. A black blotch at the base of the dorsal fin.

23. **Nemachilus butanensis.**

HAB. Bhotan. 5 inches.

Caudal fin rounded.

24. **Nemachilus griffithii.**

HAB. Assam. $5\frac{1}{2}$ inches.

Sides irregularly mottled. Several bars across the back, not extending down the sides.

25. **Nemachilus turio.**

HAB. Assam.

Body irregularly spotted and blotched.

26. **Nemachilus corica.**

HAB. Northern India.

COLOUR bluish, with a line of black blotches along the middle of the side, and smaller ones above.

27. **Nemachilus guentheri.**

HAB. Neilgherries.

Pinkish, with a network of brown markings, leaving three rows of large spots along the side.

28. **Nemachilus phoxochila.**

HAB. Upper Assam.

A dark nebulous streak along the side.

29. **Nemachilus chlorosoma.**

HAB. Upper Assam.

Straw coloured, with irregular markings.

30. **Nemachilus serpentarius.**

A wide dark chestnut band, from the snout to the base of the dorsal fin.

31. **Nemachilus blythii.**

Brownish, a dark band at the base of the caudal fin.

32. **Nemachilus evezardi.**

This species differs from the other members of the genus Nemachilus, in possessing 8 barbels.

HAB. Poona.

Caudal fin rounded. Colours greenish, with small dark blotches.

GENUS COBITIS.

CHAR. Barbels six, (or eight ?). A double erectile spine below each eye. Caudal fin rounded or square cut. Dorsal fin opposite to the ventrals.

1. **Cobitis guntea.**

HAB. India generally. 4 inches.

CHAR. Barbels well developed, origin of the dorsal fin somewhat in advance of the ventrals. Colour dirty yellowish, with a dark band along the side, and blotches down the back.

2. **Cobitis gongota.**

HAB. Assam and Bengal. 5 inches.

CHAR. Barbels short and thick. Origin of the dorsal fin above the hinder ray of the ventrals. An undulating band along the side, giving off dark bars towards the back.

I have in my collection the drawing of a fish from the base of the Khasia Hills, which stongly resembles this species in appearance, but it has 8 barbels, and the origin of the dorsal fin is well behind the ventrals.

GENUS LEPIDOCEPHALICHTHYS.

CHAR. Barbels eight. A double erectile spine beneath each eye. Caudal fin square cut. Dorsal fin nearly opposite the ventrals. The inner ray of the pectoral fin, in the adult male, is often modified into a flat spine, this is made use of to assist the fish in diving down into the mud, though this is probably not the primary object of this formation.

1. **Lepidocephalichthys thermalis.**

HAB. Southern India.

CHAR. Origin of the dorsal fin in advance of the ventrals.

COLOUR sandy, with irregular blotches along the lateral line, and others on the back. Caudal fin banded.

2. **Lepidocephalichthys balgara.**

HAB. India generally.

CHAR. Dorsal fin not in advance of the ventrals.

Back and sides irregularly mottled with brown.

GENUS BOTIA.

CHAR. Barbels six, or eight. A double erectile spine beneath each eye. Caudal fin forked.

Dorsal fin in advance of the ventrals.

1. **Botia dario.**

HAB. Northern India.

CHAR. Barbels 8. Dorsal rays 13.

Seven or eight broad brown bands, passing obliquely across the body ; ground colour yellow or white.

2. **Botia almorhæ.**

HAB. Kumaon Hill streams.

CHAR. Barbels 8. Dorsal rays 12.

Body reticulated with brown lines, leaving yellow interspaces.

3. **Botia rostrata.**

HAB. Bengal and Assam. 5 inches.

CHAR. Barbels 8. Dorsal rays 12.

Body with irregular brown crossbands, ground colour yellowish. Snout very long, pointed.

4. **Botia berdmorei.**

HAB. Bengal.

CHAR. Barbels 8. Dorsal rays 12.

COLOUR brownish, with a lead-coloured band along the side.

5. **Botia nebulosa.**

HAB. Near Darjeeling.

CHAR. Barbels 6. Dorsal rays 15.

COLOUR brownish, with a lead-coloured band along the side.

GENUS JERDONIA.

CHAR. Barbels 8. A double erectile spine beneath the eye. Dorsal fin long. The inner ray of the pectoral fin modified into a flat osseous spine.

1. **Jerdonia maculata.**

HAB. Madras.

CHAR. Dorsal rays 30. A dark lateral band from the eye to the tail. Fins yellow.

Dorsal and caudal fins banded.

GENUS ACANTHOPHTHALMUS.

CHAR. Barbels six. A small, double, erectile spine beneath the eye. Dorsal fin commences considerably behind the ventrals. Caudal fin square cut.

1. **Acanthophthalmus pangia.**

HAB. Assam and Bengal.

CHAR. Dorsal rays 8. Colour light cinnamon, without marks or bands.

We have now completed the large family of the Cyprinidæ.

We will proceed next to the Clupeidæ, or Herring family, as they are nearly related to the Cyprinidæ.

FAMILY CLUPEIDÆ. (Günth. Cat. vol. vii.)

This is also a large family, but differs from the Cyprinidæ in being essentially marine.

There are however several species which inhabit the fresh waters of India, and these I now proceed to describe. I will omit however many kinds, such as the Hilsa fish, which, though well known as an article of food in the Calcutta market, is properly a marine fish, ascending the fresh waters at certain periods of the year only for the purpose of spawning.

Char. of the Family. Body covered with scales, which are generally thin, and often easily detached. Barbels none.

Abdomen generally compressed into an edge which is often serrated. Dorsal fin rather short.

Adipose fin none. Anal fin often very long.

GENUS ENGRAULIS.

Char. Mouth very wide, upper jaw projecting.

Generally with small teeth in the jaws, on the vomer, palatine, and pterygoid bones.

Gill openings extremely wide.

Dorsal rays about 14.

1. **Engraulis purava.**

Hab. This fish is sometimes found in fresh-water tanks and rivers, but never at any great distance from the sea. "It grows to about a foot in length, is so full of bones as to be little valued, and, like many fishes of this family, dies immediately after being taken out of the water."—H. B.

CHAR. Anal rays 43 to 50. Scales 46.

Both jaws with very small teeth.

The entire abdominal edge serrated.

Anal fin commencing below the last dorsal rays.

2. **Engraulis mystax.**

CHAR. Anal rays 34. Scales 42.

Both jaws with minute teeth.

Sometimes a blackish spot across the nape.

The entire abdominal edge is serrated.

Anal fin commencing slightly behind the last ray of the dorsal.

3. **Engraulis taty.**

CHAR. Anal rays 51 to 56. Scales 46.

Both jaws with minute teeth.

Dorsal fin enveloped by scales. Anal fin commencing below the middle of the dorsal. Upper pectoral ray produced into a very long filament.

The entire abdominal edge serrated.

4. **Engraulis telara.**

HAB. Found throughout the larger rivers. It grows to the size of a small herring.

CHAR. Anal fin rays 70+75. Scales 55.

Minute teeth in both jaws.

The anal fin commences in advance of the dorsal.

Upper pectoral ray produced into a very long filament.

The entire abdominal edge serrated.

GENUS CHATOËSSUS.

CHAR. Mouth narrow, inferior, transverse.

Upper jaw projecting beyond the lower. Teeth none.

Abdomen serrated. Dorsal rays about 15.

1. **Chatoëssus manmina.**

Found in rivers and tanks. 8 inches.

CHAR. Anal rays 22 to 24. Scales 58 to 60.

A large black spot on the shoulder.

2. **Chatoëssus cortius.**

HAB. Assam.

CHAR. Anal rays 25. Scales 58.

Scales rather irregularly arranged.

This appears to be probably identical with the preceding species.

3. **Chatoëssus chanpole.**

HAB. Bengal ponds and ditches. 6 inches.

CHAR. Anal rays 21. Scales 46.

Scales arranged irregularly.

A blackish spot on the shoulder, followed by several other smaller spots.

GENUS CLUPEA.

CHAR. Upper jaw not overlapping the lower.

Teeth none, or quite rudimentary.

Abdominal serrature extending in front of the pectoral fins.

1. **Clupea chapra.**

HAB. Bengal. 6 inches.

CHAR. Dorsal rays 18. Anal 19. Scales 42.

Teeth none. Caudal fin longer than the head, covered partially with small scales, and having black margins.

2. **Clupea indica.**

HAB. Bengal and Assam.

CHAR. Dorsal rays 15. Anal 21 or 22.

Scales 80.

Teeth none. Caudal fin rather shorter than the head.

A dark spot on the shoulder.

Dr. Day considers the second of these two species to be the Clupea chapra of Buchanan. In this case I presume that the first species would have to be renamed.

GENUS CLUPEOIDES (OR CORICA).

CHAR. Lower jaw projecting beyond the upper.

Teeth none or quite rudimentary.

Abdomen serrated from behind the pectoral fins.

Anal fin with less than 20 rays.

1. **Clupeoides soborna.**

HAB. Mahanuddi River. 2 inches.

CHAR. Dorsal rays 16. Anal 15. Scales 40.

Scales very thin and transparent, colour brilliant silvery.

GENUS PELLONA.

CHAR. Lower jaw prominent. Body much compressed. Thorax and abdomen strongly serrated.

Rasplike bands of minute teeth on the palatine and pterygoid bones, and on the tongue.

Anal fin long, ventrals small. The upper ray of each pectoral fin long. Caudal fin deeply forked.

1. **Pellona motius.**

HAB. Rivers and tanks near the coast. 4 inches.

CHAR. Dorsal rays 17. Anal 39 to 45. Scales 43 to 45.

2. **Pellona dussumieri.**

CHAR. Dorsal rays 18. Anal 49 to 54. Scales 46.

GENUS MEGALOPS.

CHAR. Lower jaw projecting. Abdomen flat, not trenchant. A narrow bony plate between the mandibles. Scales large and firmly attached. Bands of viliform teeth on the jaws, vomer, and tongue, on the palatine and pterygoid bones, and the base of the skull.

1. **Megalops cyprinoides.**

HAB. Tanks near the coasts.

CHAR. Dorsal rays 17 to 20. Anal 24 to 27. Scales 37 to 42.

VII

NOTOPTERUS CHITALA.

London: L Reeve & Co.

FAMILY NOTOPTERIDÆ. (Günth. Cat. vol. vii.)

This family includes only one genus, containing a few species only, of which two are found in India, and the others in the islands of the East Indian Archipelago and in West Africa. They have some affinity to the Clupeidæ, but are only found in fresh water.

CHAR. Head and body scaly. Barbels none.

Adipose fin none. Tail tapering.

GENUS NOTOPTERUS.

Body much compressed. Abdomen with a double serrature. Scales very small. Lateral line distinct.

Both jaws with a narrow band or series of small teeth, unequal in size, bands of teeth on the vomer, palatine, and pterygoid bones, and on the sphenoid; two series of teeth on the tongue. Some of the bones of the head serrated. Anal fin very long and united with the caudal. Dorsal fin very short. Ventrals united or wanting.

1. **Notopterus chitala.**

HAB. Throughout India, rivers and tanks. Attaining according to Dr. Day, several feet in length.

CHAR. The upper profile of the the head concave.

Dorsal rays 8 to 10. Anal 110 to 125. Scales 180.

Sometimes marked with dark crossbands on the back, and with some round black occellated spots along the lower part of the tail.

2. **Notopterus kapirat.**

HAB. Throughout India. Attaining 2 feet.

CHAR. Dorsal rays 7 to 9. Anal 100 to 110. Scales 225.

Upper profile of the head scarcely concave.

COLOUR leaden, or silvery, without marks.

These fish are to be taken with bait, and are eaten by the natives. They are full of bones, however, and very indifferent as to flavour.

FAMILY SILURIDÆ. (Günth. Cat. vol. v.)

This family is a large one, and very numerously represented in Indian waters. It is (like the Cyprinidæ) essentially a fresh-water group of fishes; but some few species belonging to it are also found in salt water, keeping, however, usually near the coast.

Geographical Distribution. Members of this family are found in most tropical and temperate regions, including Africa, America, the East Indies, and Australia. One species only is found in the south-eastern parts of Europe.

Char. The Siluridæ are to be distinguished chiefly by the absence of scales; but they have sometimes bony plates on certain parts of the body.

They are provided with barbels, often of great length, and generally numerous (6 or 8).

They have frequently a second dorsal fin which is gristly, or adipose, and without rays, and their mouths are furnished with teeth, which, however, vary much in form and disposition.

GENUS CLARIAS.

Hab. Africa and the East Indies.

Char. No adipose fin. Dorsal fin long, extending from the neck to the caudal. Anal long.

Barbels 8, viz., one pair of nasal, one of maxillary, and two pairs of mandibular barbels.

Pectoral fin with a pungent spine.

1. **Clarias magur.**

Hab. India generally. Attaining 18 inches.

This is an ugly-looking, slimy fish, found in ponds and ditches, and fond of the mud; it is considered, however, by the natives to be wholesome and nourishing as food.

Char. Dorsal rays 64 to 70. Anal rays 50 to 53. The caudal fin is separate from the dorsal, and from the anal fin. The maxillary barbels reach nearly to the ends of the pectoral fins.

The pectoral spine is very finely serrated.

2. **Clarias jagur.**

Hab. Bengal. Grows to a larger size than the last species.

It is very similar to the last in appearance and habits.

Char. Dorsal rays 53. Anal rays 50.

Caudal fin united to the dorsal and the anal.

No teeth in the palate.

"Sides slightly variegated with clouds."

GENUS PLOTOSUS.

Hab. Countries bordering on the Indian Ocean.

Char. The dorsal fin is separated into two portions, a short anterior portion, with a strong spine, and a long posterior portion, which, like the anal, is confluent with the caudal. Barbels 8.

1. **Plotosus canius.**

HAB. Bengal. Grows to between 4 and 5 feet.

This fish is considered by the natives as excellent food.

"It is a long fish, somewhat of the eel form, although not quite so flexible, and is of a lurid, uniform, dark olive colour, with a tinge of violet."

CHAR. Rays of the two dorsal, the anal, and the caudal fins combined. 244 to 271.

2. **Plotosus limbatus.**

This is a doubtful species, said to differ from the last in the combined fin rays being only 224, and in the margin of the fins being black.

GENUS CHACA.

These are remarkably ugly fishes, having a wide frog mouth surrounded by numerous tentacles, and of a dirty brown or greenish colour.

CHAR. The dorsal and anal fins are each divided into two portions, the posterior portion of each being united with the caudal. The anterior portion of the dorsal fin has a strong spine. Head exceedingly large and broad. Mouth very wide. Eyes rudimentary.

1. **Chaca lophioides.**

HAB. Bengal.

CHAR. Fin rays. 1st dorsal 5; 2nd dorsal 25. Caudal 10. 2nd anal 12; 1st anal 10.

"All over the skin are scattered little fleshy projections, ragged on the surface."

2. Chaca bankanensis.

HAB. Assam.

CHAR. Fin rays. 1st dorsal 5; 2nd dorsal 22 to 24. Cadual 11. 2nd anal 11; 1st anal 12.

Head and body granular, without tentacles.

3. Chaca buchanani.

HAB. River Ganges.

CHAR. Fin rays. 1st dorsal 5; 2nd dorsal 18. Caudal 11. 2nd anal 8; 1st anal 8.

"Head and body with short tentacles, eye surrounded by a ring of small tentacles."

GENUS SACCOBRANCHUS.

This genus is restricted to the continent of India and Ceylon.

CHAR. No adipose fin. Dorsal short (7 rays).

Barbels 8, all moderately long. Pectoral fin provided with a spine.

1. Saccobranchus fossilis.

This fish is considered highly nutritious, and is much in request among the natives, as a diet for invalids.

HAB. Throughout India. 18 inches.

CHAR. Anal fin rays 68 to 79. Pectoral spine serrated.

GENUS SILURUS.

GEOGRAPHICAL DISTRIBUTION. From Germany to China.

CHAR. Barbels four or six, one pair being maxillary, and one, or two pairs, mandibular. Ventral fins with more than 8 rays. No adipose fin. Dorsal very short. Caudal rounded.

1. Silurus { berdmorei / cochinchinensis ? }

HAB. N. E. Frontier of Bengal.

CHAR. Anal rays 62. Ventrals 10. Upper jaw projects beyond the lower. Pectoral spine scarcely serrated.

Barbels four.

2. Silurus malabaricus.

HAB. Malabar.

CHAR. Anal rays 62. Ventrals 9. Lower jaw projecting.

Pectoral spine strong and serrated. Barbels 4.

3. Silurus dukai.

HAB. Sikkim.

CHAR. Anal rays 78. Pectoral spine smooth.

Anal and caudal fins united, without any distinct notch.

4. Silurus wynaadensis.

HAB. Wynaad.

CHAR. Anal rays 58 to 62. Barbels 6.

GENUS SILURICHTHYS.

CHAR. Similar to Silurus, from which it may be recognised by its having 8, or less, rays in the ventral fin. Caudal forked. Anal and caudal fins confluent.

1. **Silurichthys lamghur.**

HAB. Cashmere.

CHAR. Anal rays 53. Ventrals 6. Barbels 4. Lower jaw prominent. Pectoral spine serrated.

GENUS WALLAGO.

CHAR. Barbels 4; viz., one maxillary, and one mandibular pair.

No adipose fin. Dorsal very short. Anal fin not joining the caudal.

1. **Wallago attu.** "The Boalli."

HAB. Throughout India. Attaining sometimes as much as 6 feet in length, according to Ham. Buchanan.

This is a remarkably good fish for eating purposes, when taken from clean water, and is much in request among the natives. In Sylhet they capture it by spearing from a boat rowing slowly up stream and coming behind the fish. This would seem to indicate that it is not a bottom feeder like many of the Siluridæ. Dr. Day states, however, that it is not a cleanly feeder; and I can well imagine, being a most voracious fish, that its taste and habits are readily adapted to circumstances.

CHAR. Anal rays 86 to 93. Maxillary barbels long, nearly twice the length of the head. Pectoral spine feeble, not serrated exteriorly.

VIII

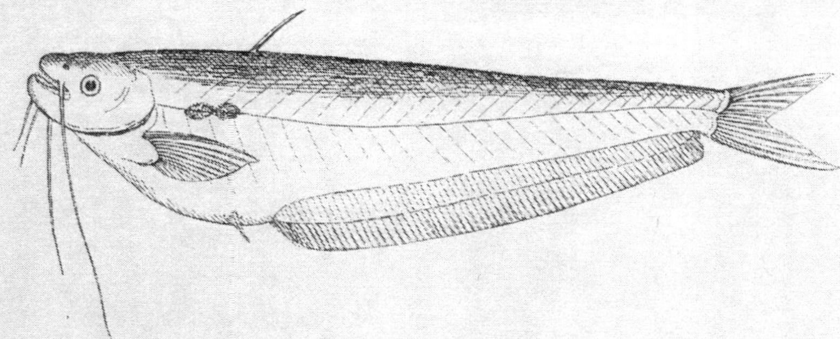

CALLICHROUS BIMACULATUS

London L. Reeve & Co.

GENUS CALLICHDOUS. "PUFTAS."

HAB. East Indies.

CHAR. No adipose fin. Dorsal very short.

Barbels 4; viz., one pair maxillary, one mandibular.

The lower jaw projects beyond the upper.

Eye behind, and partly below, the cleft of the mouth.

"They are all rich, fine-flavoured food, and grow from 9 to 12 inches in length."—H. B.

1. **Callichrous bimaculatus.**

HAB. India generally.

CHAR. Pectoral spine denticulated towards the end.

Anal rays 57 to 66.

Maxillary barbels reach to the anal fin.

A blackish blotch above the pectoral fin, at a little distance from the head.

2. **Callichrous chechra.**

HAB. Central parts of India.

The serrature of the pectoral spine varies; in some specimens I have found it stronger on the left side than on the right. In some it is hardly perceptible, and can only just be felt on passing a knife blade along the spine.

CHAR. Anal rays 67 to 73.

Maxillary barbel extends to the end of the pectoral fin. Sometimes a blackish spot just behind the gill cover. Sides clouded.

3. Callichrous pabda.

HAB. Bengal.

CHAR. Anal rays 54.

Pectoral spine smooth. Maxillary barbels long, extending to the middle of the body of the fish. Sides mottled.

A black blotch behind the gill opening and a yellow stripe along the side.

4. Callichrous anastomus.

HAB. Bengal.

CHAR. Anal rays 50 to 54.

Pectoral spine serrated. Maxillary barbels reach to the anal fin. A blackish spot behind the gill opening.

5. Callichrous canio.

HAB. Bengal and Mysore.

CHAR. Anal rays 69 to 73.

Pectoral spine smooth. Maxillary barbels extend nearly to the middle of the fish. Sides immaculate.

6. Callichrous pabo.

HAB. Assam.

CHAR. Anal rays 73.

Pectoral spine serrated. Barbels short, the maxillary ones scarcely reaching beyond the eye.

Belly red. No markings.

7. Callichrous latovittatus.

HAB. Cachar. $4\frac{1}{2}$ inches.

CHAR. Anal rays 56 to 58. Pectoral spine strongly denticulated. Maxillary barbel reaches to the end of the pectoral fin.

8. **Callichrous egertonii.**

HAB. Punjab and Sinde.

CHAR. Anal rays 52 to 54.

Pectoral spine denticulated.

Maxillary barbel reaches slightly beyond the base of the pectoral fin. Numerous dark blotches over the body.

GENUS EUTROPIICHTHYS.

CHAR. A small adipose fin. Dorsal fin short, with a spine.

Barbels 8, all short.

1. **Eutropiichthys vacha.** "The Butchua."

HAB. India generally. 1 foot.

Buchanan states that this is an excellent fish for the table. It rises readily to a fly, and affords good sport.

CHAR. Anal rays 47 to 51.

Barbels all about as long as the head.

Dorsal and pectoral spines serrated.

GENUS EUTROPIUS.

CHAR. A very small adipose fin. Dorsal fin short, with a spine. Barbels 8; viz., one to each maxillary bone, one to each posterior nostril, and two to each mandible. The mandibulary pairs are placed one behind the other.

Eutropius obtusirostris.

HAB. India.

CHAR. Anal rays 54. Maxillary barbels as long as the head, the others shorter. Dorsal and pectoral spines serrated.

GENUS PSEUDEUTROPIUS.

Char. A very small adipose fin. Dorsal fin short, with a spine. Barbels 8; viz., one pair maxillary, one between the anterior and posterior nostrils of each side, and two pairs mandibular. The mandibulary pairs are placed in a line along the front margin of the lower jaw.

Dorsal and pectoral spines serrated.

Eye situated behind the angle of the mouth, and even partly on the lower surface of the head.

1. **Pseudeutropius athernioides.**

Hab. India. 4 inches.

This is a pretty little fish, semi-transparent, and marked with three dark stripes running the length of the body and fining away on the tail.

Char. Anal rays 36 to 42. The maxillary barbels reach to the origin of the anal fin. The nasal barbels to the end of the head. Dorsal spine rather slender, slightly serrated behind. Pectoral spine stronger, armed interiorly with strong recurved teeth.

2. **Pseudeutropius mitchelli.**

Hab. Madras. $3\frac{1}{2}$ inches.

Char. Anal rays 37. The maxillary barbels reach to the ventral fins. Nasal barbels to the end of the head. Dorsal spine slender, finely serrated behind. Pectoral spine stronger, armed interiorly with strong recurved teeth.

LX

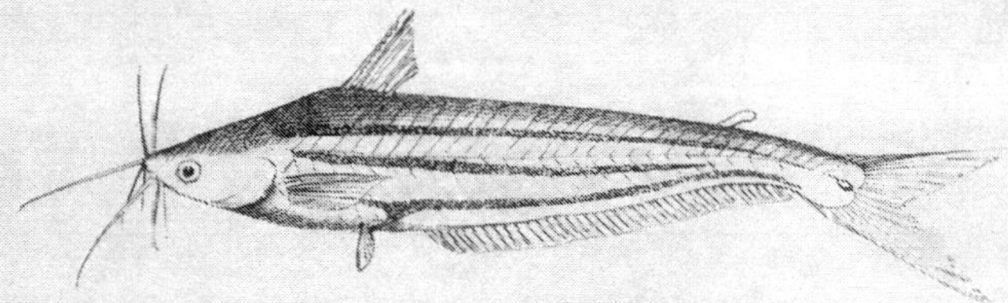

PSEUDEUTROPIUS ATHERINOIDES

London, L. Reeve & C°.

3. **Pseudeutropius megalops.**

HAB. Central India. 6 inches.

CHAR. Anal rays 41. The maxillary barbels extend beyond the origin of the anal fin; nasal barbels, to behind the eye. Dorsal and pectoral spines finely serrated on both the interior and exterior edges.

4. **Pseudeutropius longimanus.**

HAB. India. 6 inches.

CHAR. Anal rays 54. The maxillary barbels extend beyond the origin of the anal fin. Nasal barbels half as long the head. Dorsal and pectoral spines serrated interiorly, and finely granulated exteriorly.

5. **Pseudeutropius goongwaree.**

HAB. Bengal and the Deccan. 10 inches.

CHAR. Anal rays 43 to 54.

All the barbels are longer than the head. Dorsal and pectoral spines serrated interiorly.

6. **Pseudeutropius taakree.**

HAB. Orissa and the Deccan. 12 inches.

CHAR. Anal rays 51.

Maxillary barbels reach the anal fin.

7. **Pseudeutropius sykesii.**

HAB. Southern Madras and Malabar. 6 inches or more.

CHAR. Anal rays 35 to 37.

8. **Pseudeutropius murius.**

This fish is placed by Dr. Günther, doubtfully, having only Buchanan's description to go by, in the genus Eutropius.

Dr. Day, who appears to have examined specimens, says that it properly belongs to this genus.

HAB. Bengal and Orissa. 8 inches or more.

CHAR. Anal rays 39 to 43. Barbels not longer than the head. Dorsal spine nearly smooth.

GENUS SCHILBICHTHYS.

CHAR. This genus is nearly allied to Pseudeutropius. The points of difference seem to be, no adipose fin in the adult. Nostrils close together, very wide. Head covered with skin.

1. **Schilbichthys garua.**

Dr. Day remarks that the young of this species are provided with an adipose fin, which becomes altogether absorbed as the fish grows larger.

HAB. Northern India.

CHAR. Anal rays 29 to 36. 1 to 2 feet in length.

The maxillary barbels extend as far as the ventral fins. Nasal barbels short. Dorsal and pectoral spines serrated interiorly. The amount of the serrature appears to vary.

GENUS AILIA.

CHAR. Dorsal fin absent. Adipose fin very small. Barbels eight, all of them long, the mandibular pairs being placed in one line.

1. **Ailia bengalensis.**

"This small but well-flavoured fish is found throughout all the large rivers of India, excluding those of Madras and Bombay. It attains about 7 inches in length." Day.

CHAR. Anal rays 70 to 72.

2. **Ailia affinis.**

HAB. Himalayan streams.

CHAR. Anal rays 60 to 61.

Very similar to the first species, with which it seems likely that it may be identical.

GENUS AILIICHTHYS.

CHAR. Similar to Ailia, but destitute of ventral fins.

1. **Ailiichthys punctata.**

HAB. Punjab. 4 inches.

CHAR. Anal rays 76 to 82.

Upper surface of the head nearly black. A large black spot at the base of the caudal fin.

GENUS PANGASIUS.

CHAR. Adipose fin very short. Dorsal short, with a spine. Barbels slender, four; one pair maxillary, one mandibular.

1. **Pangasius buchanani.**

This is a large fish, common in the large rivers and estuaries, growing to 3 or four feet in length. It is used for food, but is not considered of the best quality.

CHAR. Anal rays 31 to 34.

Head granulated above. Dorsal and pectoral spines toothed on both edges. Barbels shorter than the head.

GENUS SILONDIA.

CHAR. Adipose fin very short. Dorsal short, with a spine.

Barbels two, minute, maxillary.

1. **Silondia gangetica.**

This is a very large fish, attaining 6 feet in length, and sometimes termed a fresh-water shark. It is usually found in the large rivers and estuaries.

CHAR. Anal rays 40 to 46.

Barbels short. Colour silvery. Fins stained with grey.

The next group have a short anal fin, and the adipose dorsal fin well developed.

GENUS MACRONES.

CHAR. The anterior and posterior nostrils separate, the latter having a pair of barbels. Adipose fin long.

Barbels eight. Pectoral fin with a serrated spine. Dorsal rays 1+7.

(a) *A separate interneural bony shield on the nape.*

1. **Macrones aor.**

HAB. Throughout India. 2 or 3 feet.

CHAR. Anal rays 13. Maxillary barbels very long, extending to the caudal fin. A black spot towards the end of the adipose fin.

X

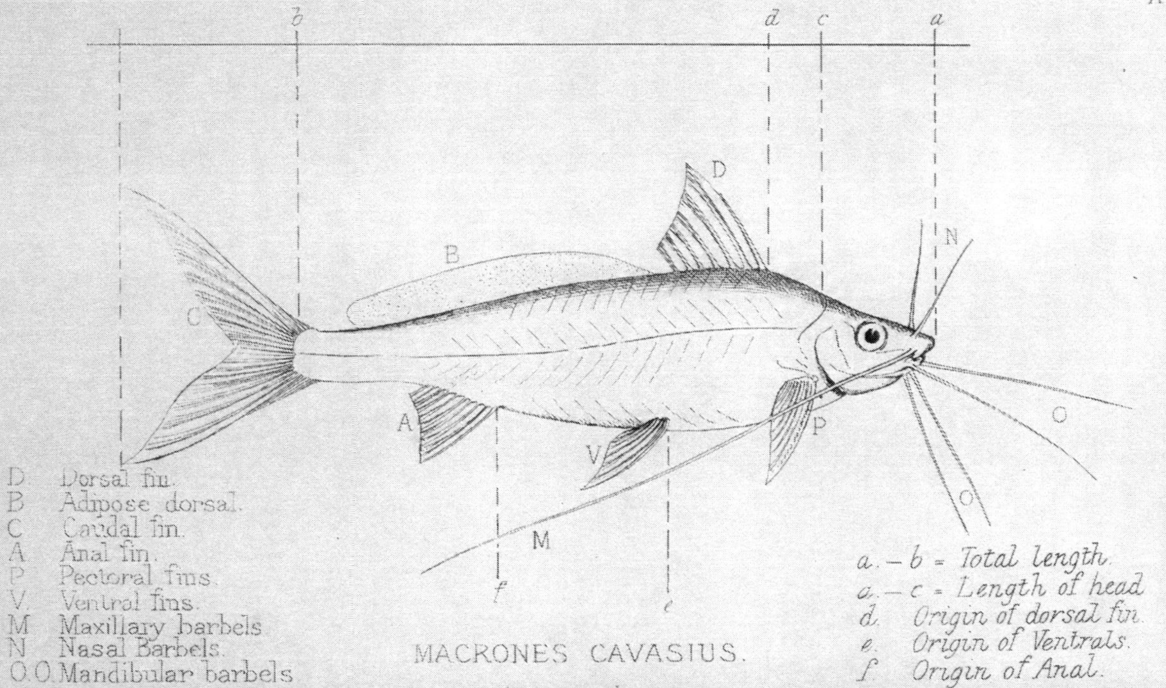

MACRONES CAVASIUS.

London L. Reeve & Co

2. Macrones lamarrii.

HAB. Northern India. 3 feet.

CHAR. Anal rays 12. Maxillary barbels reach to the end of the dorsal fin. A black spot towards the end of the adipose fin.

I have among my notes a description of another species from the Nerbudda River with anal rays 9 and without any spot on the adipose fin.

(b) *No separate shield on the nape.*

3. Macrones cavasius.

HAB. India generally. 1 foot.

CHAR. Anal rays 11. Maxillary barbels reach to the caudal fin. Dorsal spine smooth. Adipose fin very long, extending nearly the whole way from the dorsal to the caudal fin.

4. Macrones gulio.

HAB. Estuaries of large rivers. 8 inches.

Buchanan states that this fish is not very good for eating.

CHAR. Anal rays 14. Maxillary barbels reach to the anal fin. Dorsal spine strongly serrated interiorly. Adipose fin rather short.

5. Macrones tengara.

HAB. Upper India, ponds and rivers. Attaining 6 inches in length, and considered good eating.

CHAR. Anal rays 10. Maxillary barbels reach to the caudal fin. Dorsal spine smooth. Adipose fin longer than the anal. Four dark bands along the side, and a black mark above the pectoral fin.

6. **Macrones carcio.**

HAB. India generally. Attains 3 inches.

CHAR. Anal rays 12 to 14. Maxillary barbels reach the caudal fin ; the remaining barbels are shorter than the head. Dorsal spine serrated on both sides. Adipose fin short. Four dark bands along the side, and a black mark above the pectoral fin.

7. **Macrones batasio.**

HAB. River Teesta, N. Bengal. 3 inches.

CHAR. Anal rays 16. Barbels all shorter than the head. Dorsal spine smooth. Semitransparent with two longitudinal stripes, and a blackish spot on the shoulder.

8. **Macrones tengana.**

HAB. Assam and the Punjab. 3 inches.

CHAR. Anal rays 14. Barbels all shorter than the head. Dorsal spine smooth. Adipose fin short. A dark spot above the pectoral fin, and one on the top of the head. Edge of caudal fin dark, and several dark spots on the dorsal fin.

9. **Macrones keletius.**

HAB. Punjab and Bengal. Not attaining a large size.

CHAR. Anal rays 9 or 10. Maxillary barbels reach to the base of the anal fin. Dorsal spine slender and smooth.

COLOUR greyish, with two light bands along the side.

10. **Macrones chryseus.**

HAB. Western Coast. 1 foot or more.

CHAR. Anal rays 27. Barbels scarcely longer than the head. Body golden, a black blotch behind the gills.

11. **Macrones corsula.**

HAB. Lower Bengal. 1 foot or more.

CHAR. Anal rays 11 (14 ?). Maxillary barbels reach to behind the ventral fins. Dorsal spine serrated slightly. Adipose fin about as long as the anal. COLOUR brownish, with vertical rows of fine spots.

12. **Macrones punctatus.**

HAB. Madras. 18 inches.

CHAR. Anal rays 11. Maxillary barbels reach to the base of the ventral fins. Adipose fin of moderate length. About ten black spots along the lateral line.

13. **Macrones nangra.**

HAB. Ganges, and Jumna Rivers. 2 inches.

CHAR. Anal rays 9 to 11. Maxillary barbels reach to the vent. Dorsal spine smooth. Adipose fin short. Three vertical greenish bands.

14. **Macrones botius.**

HAB. Northern Bengal. 6 inches.

CHAR. Anal rays 11. Barbels all shorter than the head. Dorsal spine smooth.

COLOUR yellowish brown.

15. **Macrones vittatus.**

HAB. Malabar and Coromandel Coast.

CHAR. Anal rays 8 to 10. Maxillary barbels reach to the middle of the ventral fin. Dorsal spines serrated on both edges.

16. **Macrones malabaricus.**

HAB. Malabar.

CHAR. Anal rays 10. Maxillary barbels reach to the middle of the ventral fin. Dorsal spine smooth. Pectoral spine serrated on both edges.

A round black mark near the shoulder.

17. **Macrones oculatus.**

HAB. Southern India.

CHAR. Eye large. Anal rays 11. Maxillary barbels reach to the caudal fin. Dorsal spine serrated on both edges. Adipose fin short. Two indistinct bands along the side.

18. **Macrones cavia.**

HAB. Northern Bengal. 6 inches.

CHAR. Anal rays 9. Maxillary barbels as long as the head. Dorsal spine smooth. Adipose fin short. Two transverse bands across the tail.

GENUS RITA.

CHAR. Anterior and posterior nostrils widely separate, the latter having a pair of barbels. Barbels 6: viz., one pair maxillary, one pair mandibular, and one minute pair nasal. Dorsal rays 7. Anal 12. Dorsal and pectoral fins with very strong spines.

1. Rita crucigera.

HAB. Bengal. Grows to three or four feet in length.

CHAR. Upper surface of the head granulated, with two bony shields on the back, in front of the dorsal fin, the foremost having somewhat the shape of a cross, the hinder one of a heart shape.

A bony humeral process, above the pectoral fin, which is nearly as long as the head, and terminating in a rounded point. Dorsal spine very large, smooth on the edge. Pectoral spine strong, serrated on both edges.

2. Rita ritoides. 1 foot.

This is perhaps identical with the first species.

CHAR. Humeral process about as long as the head.

3. Rita pavimentata.

HAB. Southern India. 9 inches.

CHAR. Upper surface of the head covered with skin.

Humeral process three-fifths as long as the head, sharply pointed behind. Dorsal spine finely serrated. Pectoral spine strongly toothed on both sides.

4. Rita hastata.

CHAR. No apparent difference between this and the preceding species. Head smooth above.

5. **Rita kuturnee.**

HAB. Deccan. 6 inches.

CHAR. Maxillary barbels longer than the head. Humeral process two thirds as long as the head, narrow and rounded behind. Dorsal and pectoral spines, moderately strong, strongly serrated. Adipose fin shorter than the dorsal fin.

GENUS OLYRA.

This genus contains two small species from the Khasia Hills, but they are very insufficiently known.

CHAR. Head and body very long and low. Barbels 8. Eye small.

1. **Olyra longicaudata.**

CHAR. Anal rays 23. Pectoral spine strong, serrated on both edges. Caudal fin lanceolate.

2. **Olyra laticeps.**

CHAR. Anal rays 15, the rays becoming longer towards the hinder end of the fin. Caudal fin rounded.

GENUS ARIUS.

This genus contains many species, scattered over the tropical regions of the globe. Many of them inhabit salt water as well as fresh, some are entirely marine.

CHAR. No nasal barbels. Anterior and posterior nostrils close together. Head osseous above. Eyes with a free orbital margin. Barbels six.

1. **Arius gagorides.**

HAB. Hoogly river. 2 or 3 feet.

CHAR. Anal rays 17. Dorsal and pectoral spines granulated in front and serrated in rear.

Teeth on the palate viliform, in two pairs of confluent patches.

2. **Arius arioides.**

HAB. Bengal.

CHAR. Anal rays 21. Dorsal and pectoral spines granulated, the former slightly serrated behind.

Teeth on the palate viliform, in two broad triangular patches, joining anteriorly.

3. **Arius sona.**

HAB. Bengal.

CHAR. Anal rays 18. Maxillary barbels, and the outer mandibular pair, reach to the end of the pectoral fins when laid back. Dorsal spine indented on both edges, pectoral serrated.

4. **Arius gagora.**

HAB. Bengal. 3 feet.

CHAR. Anal rays 18 or 19. Barbels not so long as the head. Dorsal and pectoral spines indented on both edges. A large faint spot on the adipose fin. "On the palate are two bones, covered with sharp, crowded teeth."

GENUS HEMIPIMELODUS.

CHAR. No nasal barbels, anterior and posterior nostrils close together. Head osseous above. Eyes below the skin.

Barbels six.

1. Hemipimelodus peronii.

HAB. India.

CHAR. Anal rays 16. Head covered with soft skin.

Dorsal and pectoral spines strong, obscurely serrated.

Adipose fin as long as the anal.

2. Hemipimelodus viridescens.

HAB. N.W. Provinces. Small species.

CHAR. Anal rays 11 to 13.

Back reddish brown crossed by three green bars. Sides silvery. Dorsal and caudal fins spotted.

Dorsal spine not serrated. Pectoral serrated.

GENUS OSTEOGENIOSUS.

CHAR. Anterior and posterior nostrils close together.

Barbels, one pair only; maxillary, stiff and bony.

1. Osteogeniosus militaris.

HAB. River Ganges.

CHAR. Anal rays 20 to 23. The barbels extend beyond the end of the head when laid backwards.

GENUS BATRACHOCEPHALUS.

CHAR. The anterior and posterior nostrils, on each side, close together.

Barbels, one pair only, rudimentary, inserted on the chin.

1. Batrachocephalus mino.

HAB. Ganges. $1\frac{1}{2}$ feet.

CHAR. Anal rays 19. Dorsal and pectoral spines serrated on both sides. Lower jaw projecting.

The next group have, like the last, the anterior and posterior nostril on each side close together, but with a barbel between them.

GENUS BAGARIUS.

CHAR. Barbels eight. Head naked above.

1. **Bagarius yarrellii.** "The Goonch."

HAB. Large rivers of India. Attaining 6 feet in length.

This huge creature has been caught over 250 lb. in weight. H. Buchanan says of it, "It is a very ugly animal, with lurid colours." A correspondent to the 'Pioneer' wrote lately, describing the sport afforded by this fish. He says the best bait for it is the Spiny Eel or "Bahm" (*Mastacemblus armatus*). "Like most siluroids this fish will only bite from dark till about two hours after dark, when if taken his maw will invariably be found empty; and then again from dawn till 8 o'clock. It seems to feed on the young of a species of herring," (probably *Clupea chapra*).

CHAR. Anal rays 15. Maxillary barbel very broad at the base, extending beyond the end of the head.

Dorsal, pectoral, and caudal fins produced into long filaments.

Body with brown, irregular, broad cross-bands.

GENUS GLYPTOSTERNUM.

CHAR. Barbels 8. An adhesive apparatus on the throat, formed with longitudinal folds of skin.

Pectoral fins placed horizontally.

These are small fishes inhabiting mountain streams.

1. **Glyptosternum trilineatum.**

HAB. Nepal. 12 inches.

CHAR. Anal rays 13. Maxillary barbels extend to the end of the head. Dorsal spine rather slender. Pectoral spine broad, strongly toothed.

Greyish brown, with 3 light longitudinal streaks.

2. **Glyptosternum gracile.**

HAB. Nepal. 5 inches.

CHAR. Anal rays 14. Maxillary barbels extend nearly to the middle of the pectoral fin. Dorsal spine rather strong, pectoral do. very broad, both being serrated.

COLOUR brownish, fins light-coloured.

3. Glyptosternum lonah.

Hab. Deccan. 6 inches.

Char. Anal rays 11 or 12. Maxillary barbels extend to the end of the head. Dorsal spine rather slender, enveloped in skin. Pectoral spine rather broad, with a fine outer and a strong inner serrature.

Yellowish brown with dark bands. Fins yellow, with black bands.

4. Glyptosternum dekkanense.

Hab. Deccan. River Jumna. 6 inches.

Char. Anal rays 11. Maxillary barbels extend to the end of the head. Dorsal spine rather slender, enveloped in skin. Pectoral spine very broad, strongly serrated interiorly.

Colour blackish. Fins yellow, with black bands.

5. Glyptosternum striatum.

Hab. Himalayan streams. 3 or 4 inches.

Char. Anal rays 9 to 11. Maxillary barbels extend beyond the root of the pectorals. Dorsal spine slender, enveloped in skin. Adipose fin long. The outer rays of the pectoral and ventral fins are very broad, cartilaginous.

Colour brown. Fins yellow, stained with black.

6. Glyptosternum pectinopterum.

Hab. Streams near Simla.

Char. Anal rays 7. Dorsal spine with a row of sharp points along its anterior margin, the outer pectoral and ventral rays broad.

7. **Glyptosternum telchitta.**

HAB. Punjab and N.W. Provinces. 6 inches.

CHAR. Anal rays 11 to 13. Maxillary barbels short, extending to the hinder margin of the eye. Lips roughened, but not fringed. Dorsal spine smooth, pectoral spine serrated.

COLOUR reddish brown, a faint brown stripe along the side.

8. **Glyptosternum modestum.**

HAB. Punjab. 3 inches.

CHAR. Anal rays 9. Maxillary barbels nearly as long as the head.

COLOUR uniform brown.

GENUS AMBLYCEPS.

Small siluroids from the Indian continent.

CHAR. Barbels 8. Head covered with soft skin above.

Eyes very small. No adhesive apparatus on the thorax.

1. **Amblyceps tenuispinis.**

HAB. River Ganges. 2 inches.

CHAR. Anal rays 9. Barbels thin. No lateral line. Dorsal and pectoral spines short and slender. Adipose fin indistinct, and pointed posteriorly.

COLOUR olive brown.

2. **Amblyceps mangois.**

HAB. Ganges and Jumna. 4 inches.

CHAR. Anal rays 8. Barbels all longer than the head, those of the maxillaries reaching to the end of the pectoral fin. Dorsal spine smooth. No lateral line.

COLOUR olive brown.

In the remaining species of Siluridæ there is no slit across under the throat; in other words, the skin of the gill membranes is confluent with that of the central portion of the throat itself. The gill openings are thus distinctly separated the one from the other.

GENUS CALLOMYSTAX.

CHAR. Barbels eight. Anterior and posterior nostrils close together. Nasal barbels short, attached to the flap covering the posterior nostril. Eyes under the skin.

1. **Callomystax gagata.**

HAB. Bengal. 1 foot.

"It is pretty common, but is full of small bones, and of a very indifferent flavour." *H. Buchanan.*

CHAR. Anal rays 15. Maxillary barbels partially osseous, with a broad basal membrane. Dorsal spine serrated in front, smooth behind. All the fins black, with a whitish base, except the caudal which is white. Young specimens with oblique blackish bands on the back, also bands on the dorsal and caudal fins.

There are two small fishes, viz. *Phractocephalus itchkeea*, Sykes, and *Pimelodus cenia*, H. B., which may possibly turn out to be the young of this species. The latter, however, is said to be without the nasal barbels.

GENUS SISOR.

The gill openings in this group are reduced to short slits.

Pectoral and ventral fins horizontal.

CHAR. Head and trunk broad, depressed, snout long. Head partially osseous and rough. A series of bony plates along the back, from before the dorsal to the root of the caudal fin, a sharp spine taking the place of the adipose fin.

Lateral line covered with small, irregular roughnesses.

1. **Sisor rhabdophorus.**

HAB. Northern India. Attaining several feet in length.

CHAR. Anal rays 5 or 6. Maxillary barbels reach to the base of the pectoral spine, the other barbels are small and indefinite. Body and tail long. Upper ray of the caudal fin often prolonged. Dorsal ray feeble, finely serrated in front. Pectoral spine strong, with the outer edge serrated.

GENUS ERETHISTES.

CHAR. Head broad, covered with bony plates. Tail narrow. Mouth small. Dorsal fin with a strong serrated spine. Anal with about 10 rays. Body with minute tubercles arranged in longitudinal series. Eyes small.

1. **Erethistes pusillus.**

HAB. Assam. 2 inches.

CHAR. Dorsal and pectoral spines very strong.

2. **Erethistes hara.** (*Hara buchanani*, Günth.)

HAB. Bengal and Assam. 2½ inches.

CHAR. Dorsal and pectoral spines of moderate strength, the former serrated interiorly, the latter with strong teeth internally, and double spines, pointing forwards and backwards, on the exterior edge.

COLOUR brown, banded.

3. **Erethistes conta.**

HAB. Lower Bengal. 4 inches.

CHAR. Dorsal spine serrated interiorly, pectoral spine toothed on both sides, the teeth on the outside pointing forwards. Barbels shorter than the head.

COLOUR brown, fins spotted.

4. **Erethistes jerdoni.**

HAB. Sylhet. 1 inch.

CHAR. The pectoral spine toothed as in E. conta, the remaining rays of the pectoral fin are rudimentary, and scarcely perceptible.

5. **Erethistes elongata.**

HAB. Naga Hills.

GENUS PSEUDECHENEÏS.

CHAR. Barbels eight. Head covered with soft skin. Mouth small. An adhesive apparatus on the thorax, differing from that of Glyptosternum in having the plaits of skin transverse instead of longitudinal. Gill opening small. Pectoral and ventral fins placed horizontally.

1. **Pseudecheneïs sulcatus.**

HAB. Mountain streams of N. E. Bengal. 5½ inches.

CHAR. Anal rays 11. Outer rays of the pectoral and ventral fins broad and flexible, striated beneath. Dorsal spine flexible.

Mottled with brown and yellow.

GENUS EXOSTOMA.

CHAR. Adipose fin long. Barbels 6 or 8. Lips formed into a broad flat sucker round the mouth. Gill openings very small.

1. **Exostoma labiatum.**

HAB. Mishmee Hills, Assam. 3½ inches.

CHAR. Maxillary barbels extend to the base of the pectoral fin.

2. **Exostoma blythii.**

HAB. Sikkim Hill streams. 3 inches.

CHAR. Maxillary barbels rudimentary.

COLOUR yellowish brown.

FAMILY SCOMBRESOCIDÆ. (Günth. Cat. vol. vi.)

This is essentially a marine family, spread over all the temperate and tropical regions. The species, however, noted below are found in the Indian fresh waters, and the first is tolerably abundant. This family includes the genus *Exocœtus* or flying fish.

CHAR. Rayed dorsal fin opposite the anal. No adipose fin. Body covered with scales.

GENUS BELONE.

CHAR. Both jaws prolonged into a long slender beak, provided with pointed teeth. Body elongate, slender, covered with small scales.

1. **Belone cancila**. (Kangkila.)

This is very similar to the Gar fish, which is common off the British coasts, and is often taken in mackerel nets. Both species are well flavoured.

It is a voracious fish, and may be easily caught with a bait or with a fly; it usually swims near the surface.

HAB. Ponds and rivers. 1 foot.

CHAR. Dorsal rays 16 or 17. Anal 17 or 18.

GENUS HEMIRAMPHUS.

CHAR. Lower jaw only elongated like a beak. Teeth viliform in both jaws.

1. **Hemiramphus ectuntio.**

HAB. Rivers and ponds Bengal and Orissa. 1 foot.

CHAR. Dorsal rays 13. Anal 11. Scales 52? A ridge along the side. Scales fall off easily. On each side a broad, silvery, longitudinal stripe.

2. **Hemiramphus brachynotopterus.**

HAB. Hoogly.

CHAR. Dorsal 9. Anal 15.

FAMILY CYPRINODONTIDÆ.

(Günth. Cat. vol. vi.)

Fresh-water fish of temperate and tropical regions.

CHAR. Head and body covered with scales. Adipose fin none. Barbels none. Teeth in both jaws.

GENUS CYPRINODON.

CHAR. Teeth in a single series, incisor-like, notched. Origin of dorsal fin in advance of that of the anal.

Colouration of sexes often different.

1. **Cyprinodon stolickanus.**

HAB. Cutch. Small species.

CHAR. Dorsal 9. Anal 9. Scales 27.

GENUS HAPLOCHILUS.

CHAR. Teeth in narrow bands, pointed. Dorsal commencing behind the anal.

1. **Haplochilus panchax.**

HAB. Bengal. Attaining 2 or 3 inches.

CHAR. Dorsal 6 to 8. Anal 14 to 16. Scales 30 to 34.

A bright silvery spot on the head, a second near the dorsal fin, a dark mark at the base of the dorsal, and a dark edging to the caudal fin.

2. **Haplochilus melastigmus.**

HAB. Bengal. 1 inch.

CHAR. Dorsal 7. Anal 22. Ventral fins very minute. A black spot at the base of the dorsal. Teeth slightly hooked.

3. **Haplochilus rubrostigma.**

HAB. Madras and Sind. Small species.

CHAR. Dorsal 8. Anal 14–15. "Numerous brilliant blue spots on the body, alternating with rusty red ones along the sides." *Day.*

4. **Haplochilus argenteus.**

HAB. Madras. 1½ inches.

CHAR. Dorsal 6. Anal 14. Scales 27.

5. **Haplochilus lineatus.**

HAB. Coorg and Malabar. 4 inches.

CHAR. Dorsal 8 or 9. Anal 15 or 16. Scales 32 to 34.

A green spot on each scale. Body banded. Fins tipped with red.

The only remaining families of PHYSOSTOMI to be considered are the *Symbranchidæ* and *Murænidæ* or Eels. These do not, however, include the spiny eels or *Mastacembelidæ*, which will be found in another division.

FAMILY SYMBRANCHIDÆ.

(Günth. Cat. vol. viii.)

CHAR. Body long, snake-like, with or without minute scales. No pectoral or ventral fins. Vertical fins rudimentary, reduced to mere folds of skin. Only one aperture to the gills, situated on the lower surface.

GENUS AMPHIPNOUS.

CHAR. Palatine teeth in a single series. Small scales on the body, arranged longitudinally.

1. **Amphipnous cuchia.**

HAB. Bengal, near the coast. 2 feet or more.

CHAR. No apparent fins.

COLOUR above dark green, below a dirty pale red. On every part are scattered small round black spots, and short yellowish lines.

Body slimy, the scales not being apparent.

This eel, having no fins, is very similar in appearance to a snake. It is fond of lying in the grass near the water, but on being disturbed takes to the water at once. The natives catch them with wicker baskets, open at the ends, which they place over them as they are trying to reach the water.

GENUS SYMBRANCHUS.

CHAR. Palatine teeth in a band. Scales absent.

1. **Symbranchus bengalensis.**

HAB. Lower Bengal and coast districts.

CHAR. Snout very short, eyes small, close to the end of the snout.

FAMILY MURÆNIDÆ. (Günth. Cat. vol. viii.)

CHAR. Body naked, or with rudimentary scales.

Ventral fins none, vertical fins united one with the other, without spines.

GENUS ANGUILLA.

CHAR. End of the tail surrounded by the fin, tongue free, nostrils superior or lateral, pectoral fins present. Skin with rudimentary scales.

1. **Anguilla bengalensis.**

Very similar to the common eel of Europe. It is found throughout India, generally in marshes, and is a very foul feeder.

2. **Anguilla bicolor.**

HAB. Lower provinces of Bengal and Madras.

I am not acquainted with the distinctive peculiarities of these two species.

GENUS OPHICHTHYS.

CHAR. End of tail free, nostrils labial, tongue tied down, pectoral fins small, dorsal and anal fins very long.

1. **Ophichthys hyala.**

HAB. Rivers of Bengal both salt and fresh. 18 inches.

Upper parts dotted with minute green spots. A row of pale round spots along the lateral line. The natives have a superstition that this fish proceeds from the ear of the porpoise.

GENUS MORINGUA.

CHAR. Tail much shorter than the trunk, pectorals none or small, vertical fins only developed towards the end of the tail. No scales.

1. **Moringua raitaborua.**

HAB. Bengal.

COLOUR above purple with black dots. Dorsal and anal fins interrupted in the middle, the hinder portion of each being joined into one fin. It grows to the length of nearly two feet.

We have now completed the Fishes of the great order PHYSOSTOMI.

There is one peculiar little fish which I will here notice, as it is found in fresh water. It belongs to the

ORDER LOPHOBRANCHII.

CHAR. Gills not laminated, but composed of small rounded lobes, attached to the branchial arches. Body covered with an armour of bony plates. Snout produced, mouth small, toothless.

FAMILY SYNGNATHIDÆ. (Günth. Cat. vol. viii.)

CHAR. Gill opening very small, situated near the upper angle of the gill cover. One soft dorsal fin, no ventrals.

GENUS DORYICHTHYS.

CHAR. Pectoral and caudal fins present, body with prominent ridges. The male has a pouch on the abdomen for carrying the eggs after they are deposited by the female.

1. **Doryichthys deocata.**

HAB. Rivers of Northern Bengal.

COLOUR brown, with the sides of the belly beautifully variegated with red and blue.

A very small mouth situated at the extremity of a long tube.

There are several other species of Pipe fishes found in the estuaries of Indian rivers, but, as they appear to be strictly speaking marine species, are not included within the scope of the present work.

The Tetrodons are most eccentric-looking little creatures with round bodies, which when taken out of the water they inflate suddenly with air, till they have the appearance of a bladder.

They belong to the

ORDER PLECTOGNATHI.

CHAR. Mouth narrow, the bones of the upper jaw united, sometimes produced into the form of a beak.

FAMILY GYMNODONTES. (Günth. Cat. vol. viii.)

CHAR. Body rounded. One dorsal fin without spines. No ventral fins. Jaw bones forming a beak with a sharp edge. No teeth.

GENUS TETRODON.

CHAR. Each jaw divided in the middle, forming an appearance of four teeth. Dorsal and anal fins very short. Body inflatable, sometimes covered with spines.

1. **Tetrodon patoca.**

HAB. Coasts and rivers. 13 inches.

Back and abdomen densely covered with very small spines.

Upper parts brown, with white or yellowish spots.

Dorsal 11. Pectoral 16. Anal 10. Caudal 10.

2. Tetrodon cutcutia.

HAB. Coasts and rivers. 4 inches.

Body smooth. Green above, sides with a network of brownish lines. A large black spot edged with white is usually present on the side in advance of the dorsal fin.

Dorsal 12. Pectoral 21. Anal 11. Caudal 8.

3. Tetrodon fluviatilis.

HAB. Coast and fresh waters. 6 or 7 inches.

CHAR. Body apparently smooth, but the head, back, and belly are armed with small prickles, which can be retracted beneath the skin.

Upper parts greenish with irregular roundish dark blotches, lower parts uniform whitish or dark coloured.

Dorsal 16. Pectoral 17. Anal 14. Caudal 8.

I will next take into consideration the large and important

ORDER ACANTHOPTERYGII,

or spiny rayed fishes.

In most systematic works this order is placed first, it does not, however, occupy such an important place among the Indian fresh-water fishes as it does in other parts of the world, and for this reason I have placed them after the Physostomi.

They are to be distinguished by having a number of the rays of the dorsal and anal fins and often the first ray of the ventral composed of strong sharp spines. They have frequently two dorsal fins, but both of them are composed of rays, and the adipose, or gristly, fin does not appear in this order. When there are two dorsal fins, the first is composed entirely of spinous rays, or the two fins may be united. The Ophiocephalidæ appear at first sight to be exceptions to the general rule, inasmuch as they have no spinous rays in any of their fins. There is no doubt, however, of their belonging to this order, and we may conclude, as occurs in some other cases, that the first dorsal fin is wanting, or perhaps on account of their burrowing habits, the soft portions of their fins may have become developed at the expense of the spiny rays.

FAMILY PERCIDÆ. (Günth. Cat. vol. i.)

This family, of which the European Perch is the type, are carnivorous fishes, and are found in the seas and fresh waters of all parts of the globe. The only representatives of the family in Indian fresh waters are small fishes belonging to the

GENUS AMBASSIS.

CHAR. All the teeth viliform, two dorsal fins. Scales large, deciduous. Præoperculum with a double toothed edge, the first dorsal with seven, the anal with three spines, a recumbent spine in front of the dorsal pointing forwards.

They are all small fishes, with the body deep and compressed, more or less transparent.

1. **Ambassis nalua.**

HAB. Bengal. Body deep in proportion to its length.

Fin rays. Second dorsal 1+10 or 11. Anal 3+10. Scales large, about 30.

2. **Ambassis ranga.**

HAB. Bengal and Madras. $1\frac{1}{2}$ inches. Body deep.

Fin rays. Second dorsal 1 + 12 to 14. Anal 3 + 13 to 15. Scales small, 58.

3. **Ambassis baculis.**

HAB. Throughout India.

Dorsal 1 + 13. Anal 3 + 13. Scales absent or very minute.

4. **Ambassis lata.**

HAB. Bengal and N.W. Provinces.

Fin rays. Second dorsal 1 + 12 to 14. Anal 3 + 15. Scales small.

COLOUR, in the adult, golden, with orange dots, the sides have several transverse bars alternately of dusky and of gold, with a green gloss.

5. **Ambassis nama.**

HAB. Throughout India. Attaining 3 or 4 inches in length.

This differs from the preceding 4 species in having a longer body.

Fin rays. Second dorsal 1 + 14 to 16. Anal 3 + 13 to 17.

Scales none, or excessively minute.

6. **Ambassis thomassi.**

HAB. Western coast.

Second dorsal 1 + 11. Anal 3 + 10.

Scales 38. Appears, from the description, to be very similar to A. nalua.

XI

AMBASSIS RANGA.

AMBASSIS NAMA.

London. L. Reeve & Co

FAMILY GOBIIDÆ. (Günth. Cat. vol. iii.)

CHAR. Body elongate. Two dorsal fins, the spinous portion being always the less developed, and composed of flexible spines.

The Gobies are carnivorous fishes, living in the fresh waters and off the coasts of temperate and tropical regions. They reside mostly at the bottom of the water.

GENUS GOBIUS.

CHAR. Both ventrals united into one disk-shaped fin.

Body scaly, teeth conical, those of the upper jaw in several series.

1. Gobius giuris.

HAB. Found on all the East Indian coasts and fresh waters.

This fish is common all over India, it is much in request for food, being light and well-flavoured. It grows to about a foot, or $1\frac{1}{2}$ feet in length.

COLOUR greenish, with irregular cloudy blotches.

Fins spotted.

Dorsal fin rays 6 + (1 + 9). Anal 1 + 8. Scales 26 to 34.

2. Gobius malabaricus.

HAB. Madras and Malabar, small species.

COLOUR brown with a black crescentic, white edged mark, on the first dorsal fin.

Dorsal rays 6 + (1 + 10.) Anal 11. Scales 50.

GENUS EUCTENOGOBIUS.

CHAR. Teeth of the upper jaw in one row.

1. **Euctenogobius striatus.**

HAB. Lower districts of Southern India. 6 inches.

COLOUR buff, with some vertical bands.

Dorsal rays 6 + (1 + 10.) Anal 11. Scales 54.

FAMILY NANDIDÆ. (Günth. Cat. vol. iii.)

CHAR. Body oblong, compressed, covered with scales. Lateral line interrupted. Dorsal fins united, the spiny portion being more developed than the soft.

GENUS BADIS.

CHAR. None of the bones of the head armed.

1. Badis buchanani.

HAB. Throughout India, except in Madras. 3 inches.

Fin rays. Dorsal 17 + 8. Anal 3 + 7. Scales 28 to 30.

COLOUR dark, either greenish or purplish black, sometimes banded. A small round blue spot on the shoulder.

2. Badis dario.

HAB. Bengal and Behar. 3 inches.

COLOUR silvery, with black transverse belts, but in dirty water the black colour extends all over the body.

Dorsal rays 14 + 8. Anal 3 + 7. Scales 26.

GENUS NANDUS.

CHAR. Præoperculum serrated, operculum with one or two spines.

1. **Nandus marmoratus.**

HAB. Throughout India. 6 inches.

General colour pale green, with a silvery gloss, on which are scattered many large irregular marks of a dark colour, inclining to olive.

Dorsal rays 13 + 12. Anal 3 + 7. Scales 46 to 57.

FAMILY LABYRINTHICI. (Günth. Cat. vol. iii.)

CHAR. Head covered with scales, teeth small. Gill opening rather narrow. A superbranchial organ, composed of thin laminæ, situated in a cavity above the gills. The fishes of this family are remarkable for the length of time they can exist out of the water. The peculiar apparatus with which their gills are provided, seems to enable them to breathe as well, or better, out of the water as in it.

GENUS ANABAS.

CHAR. Præorbital and opercles serrated. Lateral line interrupted.

1. **Anabas scandens.**

HAB. India generally, near the coast. 6 inches.

This fish is most remarkable for its powers of living in the air. The fishermen keep them for five or six days in an earthen pot or covered basket. If in a basket, it is necessary to keep it securely covered, as they can climb up the sides and escape with the greatest ease. They can travel a long distance on land, on occasions when the water they are living in becomes stagnant or dried up, and they can also, in common with several other Indian fishes, remain in a semi-torpid condition under the mud for months together. Hence they are often found after a heavy storm in places where they would the least be expected, and have frequently been accused of falling from the clouds.

CHAR. Dorsal rays 17 or 18 + 8 to 10. Anal 10 + 10. Scales 28 to 32.

COLOUR varies, sometimes marked with dark bands.

GENUS POLYACANTHUS.

CHAR. Mouth small, and but little protractile. Opercles without spines.

1. Polyacanthus cupanus.

HAB. Madras, near the coasts. 3 inches.

CHAR. Dorsal fin rays. 14 to 16 spinous + 5 to 7 soft rays and 16 to 19 spinous + 10 to 11 soft. Scales 29 to 32.

COLOUR. greenish, fins barred, with a dark spot at the base of the caudal. Ventral fin with an elongated ray, which is scarlet.

GENUS OSPHROMENUS.

CHAR. Operculum without spines, but finely serrated in the young. Ventral fins with the outer ray very long, filiform, the remaining rays being small and rudimentary.

1. Osphromenus nobilis.

HAB. A small fish found in the N. E. of Bengal.

CHAR. Two white bands along the sides, and a third along the base of the anal fin. Dorsal rays 5 or 6 + 7 or 8. Anal 5 + 23. Scales 28 to 30.

GENUS TRICHOGASTER.

Char. Operculum without serrature. Mouth small, oblique, slightly protractile. Ventral fins reduced to a single long hair-like ray.

1. **Trichogaster fasciatus.**

Hab. India generally, excepting southern and western Madras. Grows to 5 inches.

Char. Dorsal rays from 23 to 28, of which 14 to 17 are spinous. Anal rays from 29 to 33, of which 15 to 18 are spinous. A sharp spine under the eye.

The colouration appears to vary, but is always brilliant. Usually greenish, with oblique crossbands, often beautifully variegated with red, yellow, or blue.

These little fish are admirably adapted for an aquarium, and are easily kept. Buchanan described six varieties as distinct, most of which appear to belong to this species. The following species, however, seems to be distinct, and some of the others may possibly turn out to be so.

2. **Trichogaster chuna.**

Hab. Bengal. $1\frac{1}{2}$ inches.

Char. Dorsal rays 24, of which 17 are spinous. Anal rays 30, of which 19 are spinous.

A broad black stripe running from the eye to the end of the tail. Head unarmed.

FAMILY MUGILIDÆ. (Günth. Cat. vol. iii.)

Char. Two short dorsal fins, the anterior with four spines. Cleft of the mouth not wide, the corners of the mouth being bent angularly inwards. Without teeth, or with feeble teeth. Gill opening wide.

Fresh waters and coasts of all the temperate and tropical regions. Feeding on soft organic substances or very small animals.

These are the Grey Mullet. They are not to be confounded, however, with the Red Mullets, which belong to a very distinct family.

GENUS MUGIL.

Char. No true teeth in the jaws.

1. **Mugil nepalensis.**

Hab. Nepal. 8 inches.

Char. Scales 29. Depth of body contained 5 times in the total length (inclusive of the caudal fin).

2. **Mugil parsia.**

Hab. Northern India. 6 inches.

Char. Scales 35. Depth contained 4½ times.

3. **Mugil cantoris.**

Hab. Hoogly.

Char. Scales 33. Depth contained 4½ times.

4. Mugil corsula.

HAB. Bengal and N. W. Provinces. 1 foot.

CHAR. Scales 49 to 52. Depth contained 6 times in the total. Head rising higher than the back. Eyes protuberant. Sides with rows of dark dots.

This is one of the most delicious of Indian fish. They are to be met with in jheels and deep streams, and are seen swimming in shoals, their eyes only showing above water; they are difficult to catch, as they dart along the surface when disturbed, and leap over any net or other obstruction, and they will not take any kind of bait. The best way to secure them is to shoot them with small shot, waiting for them patiently and quietly on the high bank, and firing into the middle of the shoal. It is necessary to have a boat in readiness if the water is deep, as they are apt to sink immediately they are killed. It will be found that a little trouble and patience is well repaid when dinner time arrives. They should be cooked as soon as possible after they leave the water.

5. Mugil cascasia.

HAB. Upper India. 3 or 4 inches.

Yellow marks on the base of the caudal and pectoral fins, also on the chin and eye. Scales 32.

FAMILY OPHIOCEPHALIDÆ.

(Günth. Cat. vol. iii.)

(Or snake-headed fishes.)

Are found only in the East Indies. They are a fresh-water family, and of carnivorous habits.

Like the Labyrinthici they are able to exist for a long time out of the water, they afford a light and wholesome but rather insipid diet. They are long in shape, with a large mouth, the head and body being covered with scales. They have long dorsal and anal fins, without any spines, teeth in the jaws, and on the palate.

1. **Ophiocephalus punctatus.**

HAB. India generally, in ponds. 1 foot.

CHAR. This fish is not considered so good for eating as *O. striatus*.

COLOUR dirty green, with a dark stripe, and dark bars. Black dots scattered over the lower half of the body.

Scales 40. Dorsal rays 29 to 32. Anal 20 to 22.

2. **Ophiocephalus gachua.**

HAB. India generally. 8 inches to 1 foot.

COLOUR above greenish with several indistinct bands descending obliquely forwards from the back to the lateral line. Pectoral fin with transverse bars.

CHAR. Scales 40 to 46. Dorsal rays 34 to 37. Anal 21 to 23.

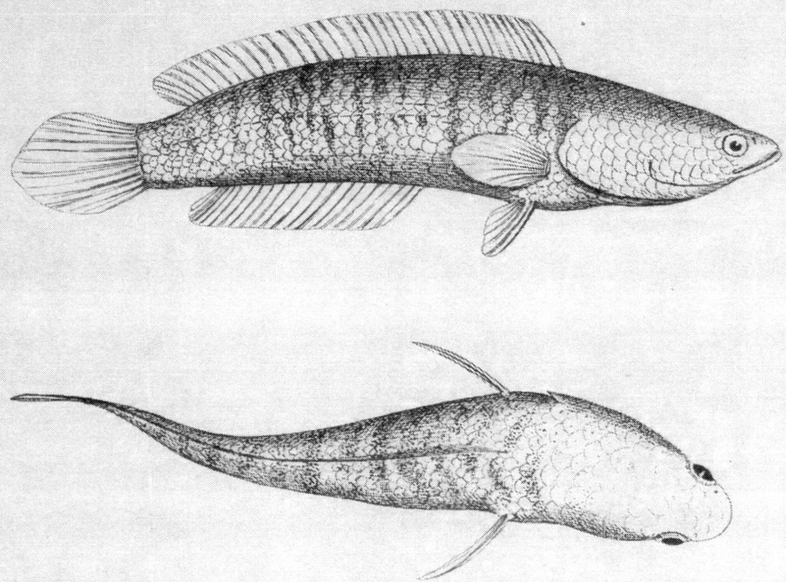

OPHIOCEPHALUS PUNCTATUS.

London: L. Reeve & Co.

3. **Ophiocephalus stewartii.**

HAB. Assam. 10 inches.

CHAR. Scales 50. Dorsal rays 39–40. Anal 27.

4. **Ophiocephalus striatus.**

HAB. Throughout India. 2 or 3 feet.

This fish is considered the best for eating of the genus, and affords good sport, and may be taken by spinning: the most killing way, however, is to put down night-lines baited with frogs; care must be taken or the frogs will be found in the morning, each seated safely on a weed or stone clear out of the water.

COLOUR dark grey above, with dark bands down the body.

CHAR. Scales 51 to 57. Dorsal rays 37 to 45. Anal 22 to 27.

5. **Ophiocephalus barca.**

HAB. Bengal. 3 feet.

An ugly fish, living mostly in holes burrowed in the banks of rivers; considered very good eating.

COLOURS dark green, sides yellow, body covered thickly with irregular black spots, with a few red ones.

CHAR. Scales 62. Dorsal rays 50 to 52. Anal 35 to 36.

6. **Ophiocephalus marulius.** "The Murrel."

HAB. Throughout India. 3 or 4 feet.

COLOURS vary, but there is always an eye-like spot on the caudal fin, in adult specimens, with about five large irregular dark marks along the side below the lateral line.

CHAR. Scales 59 to 64. Dorsal rays 48 to 55. Anal 31 to 36. Depth of body contained 7 times in total length. 4 rows of scales between the back and the anterior portion of the lateral line, which is distinct.

7. **Ophiocephalus pseudomarulius.**

Very similar to the last, but not so long in proportion to the depth; apparently without spots on the side, but having the ocellus on the tail fin.

CHAR. Scales 64. Dorsal rays 47. Anal 33. 6 rows of scales between the back and the anterior portion of the lateral line, which is distinct.

8. **Ophiocephalus diplogramme.**

HAB. Western coast. $1\frac{1}{2}$ feet.

"Two horizontal black iateral bands."

CHAR. Scales 112. Dorsal rays 43. Anal 27.

FAMILY MASTACEMBELIDÆ.

(Günth. Cat. vol. iii.)

(Spiny Eels.)

CHAR. Body long, with very small scales. Dorsal fin very long, the anterior portion composed of numerous separate spines. No ventral fins.

GENUS RHYNCHOBDELLA.

CHAR. Head elongate, upper jaw pointed, and terminating in a long fleshy appendage, which is striated beneath. Præoperculum without any spines.

1. **Rhynchobdella aculeata.**

HAB. India generally. 1 foot in length.

From two to nine black, white-edged ocelli along the base of the hinder dorsal fin.

CHAR. Dorsal spines 16 to 20. Fin rays 48 to 55. Anal 3 spines, and 44 to 58 soft rays.

GENUS MASTACEMBLUS.

CHAR. Upper jaw with a long movable appendage which is not striated beneath. Præoperculum with spinous teeth at the angle.

1. **Mastacemblus pancalus.**

HAB. Throughout India. 6 inches.

CHAR. The caudal fin is separate from the dorsal and anal. Dorsal spines 24 to 26, soft rays 30 to 40. Anal 3+31 to 44.

COLOUR above green, marked with black and white dots on the body and fins.

2. **Mastacemblus armatus.**

HAB. Throughout India. 2 feet.

CHAR. The caudal fin is continuous with the dorsal and anal. Dorsal spines 35 to 39. Fin rays 74 to 87. Anal 3 spines, and 79 to 87 soft rays.

COLOUR brownish olive, variegated with spots or zigzag stripes and bands.

3. **Mastacemblus aleppensis.**

HAB. Bhotan. 18 inches.

CHAR. Dorsal spines 32 to 35. Fin rays 80. Anal 3 + 80. Sometimes a notch between the vertical fins.

COLOUR blackish, variegated with yellow.

4. **Mastacemblus guentheri.**

HAB. Malabar. 7 inches.

CHAR. Horizontal limb of præoperculum serrated.

COLOURS marbled.

CHAR. Dorsal spines 27–28. Fin rays 60–64. Anal 3 + 62 to 64.

There are two species remaining to be noticed which belong to a different Order. It will be sufficient, however, to mention the characteristics of the Family.

FAMILY CHROMIDES. (Günth. Cat. vol. iv)

CHAR. Dorsal fin single, the spinous portion usually of greater extent than the soft, and with three or more spines.

Colouration brilliant.

GENUS EUTROPLUS.

CHAR. Body elevated and compressed. Teeth in two rows in the jaws. Lateral line interrupted or abruptly ceasing.

1. **Eutroplus suratensis.**

HAB. Malabar and Coromandel coast. 1 foot.

Found in tanks not far from the sea.

COLOUR green or purple, with eight vertical bands.

CHAR. Scales 45.

2. **Eutroplus maculatus.**

HAB. Madras and Malabar. 3 inches.

COLOUR canary yellow, with seventeen horizontal rows of golden spots, and three dark blotches along the middle of the side.

CHAR. Scales 35.

APPENDIX TO CHAPTER V.

A few species remain still to be noticed, which I have purposely omitted hitherto, on account either of their being so slightly known or insufficiently described, that their position is doubtful, or else of there being some uncertainty as to their being distinct species or only varieties. In most of these cases it will be observed that they are known only from description, there being no specimens in the British Museum to refer to.

Barbus chrysopoma, Cuv.

Dr. Day considers this the same as *Barbus sarana.*

HAB. Poona.

CHAR. Scales 29, transverse $5 + 4\frac{1}{2}$. Body strongly compressed, somewhat elevated.

Generally a large blackish blotch on the side of the end of the tail.

Barbus russellii, Günther.

Dr. Day considers this to be a variety of *Barbus pinnauratus.*

There are two specimens from the river Indus at Sabzilkot in the British Museum collection, length 5 inches.

HAB. Western and southern parts of India.

It appears to be without the black spot on the tail, otherwise there seems little to distinguish it from *Barbus pinnauratus.*

Barbus polydori, Cuv.

No specimens in the British Museum.

HAB. Bombay.

CHAR. Barbels 4. Dorsal ray slender and finely serrated.

Colouration uniform.

Dorsal rays 12. Scales 27.

Barbus liacanthus, Bkr.

Dr. Day considers this fish to be the same as *Barbus chola.* It was described by Bleeker from specimens collected in Java, and it seems very possible that the single species from Cochin in the British Museum may belong to *Barbus chola*, and that the Java species may be distinct. My reason for making this suggestion is that I perceive that the British Museum has no specimen of *Barbus chola* which is a common species in India. However, I am not in a position to judge definitely on this question.

Barbus sophoroides, Günther.

Here again is a disputed species, which Dr. Day considers to be a variety of *Barbus chola.*

HAB. Bengal, Cachar. 3 inches.

It has a black spot across the base of the *middle* dorsal rays (as well as one on the tail). *B. chola* has frequently a dark mark at the base of the *anterior* dorsal rays, besides irregular spots on the fin (and a spot on the tail).

Barbus hamiltonii, Day.

Described first by Dr. Day in his Fish of Malabar. He seems since to have had reason to consider it only a variety of *B. chola.* The apparent distinctions are: scales 24; barbels short. No dark mark on the dorsal fin.

Leuciscus presbyter, Cuv.

A doubtful species, perhaps belonging to genus Barbus.

HAB. Bombay.

CHAR. Barbels none. Dorsal ray weak, not bony. Scales 26. Lateral line concave.

Dorsal fin slightly edged with black.

Oreinus progastus, M'Clelland.

HAB. Upper Assam where it is called the "Adoee."

"Found chiefly in rivers, along the borders of Assam, where the stream is rapid enough to prevent any kind of navigation with boats or canoes. It attains 6 or 8 pounds in weight. It is not fit to eat, as it occasions swimming of the head and temporary loss of reason for several days. It is to be recognised by its lengthened and fleshy snout."

It is impossible to tell from the description alone whether this is a distinct species, or identical with either of those already described.

Labeo leschenaultii, Cuv.

Very similar to, if not identical with Labeo fimbriatus. There would appear to be two specimens in the British Museum, one from a tank in South Arcot, the other from Central Asia. The distinctive points are as follows: Scales 43 to 44, transverse 9 + 8.

5½ series between the lateral line and the ventral fin.

Cyprinus nancar, H. Buchanan.

Hab. Small rivers of the Gorruckpore district. 3 lbs.

Description. Dorsal rays 20. Anal 8. Barbels 4, minute edges of the lips smooth. Scales large. (By this term Buchanan would probably mean to indicate from 35 to 40.) Mouth low, extends straight back and is small. The jaws protrude in opening. Back sharp edged.

Colour above dark green, with a golden gloss. Fins dark coloured. Eyes reddish.

This fish may perhaps be a Labeo, but its position is very doubtful, until some one shall procure specimens.

Chondrostoma boggut, Sykes.

Perhaps the same as Labeo striolatus.

Hab. Deccan, Central India.

Char. Dorsal rays 12 or 13. Scales 60 to 65, transverse 12 + 14. One pair of maxillary barbels.

Chondrostoma mullya, Sykes.

Probably a Labeo.

HAB. Beema River, Deccan. 6 inches.

CHAR. Dorsal rays 11. Anal 8.

COLOUR dark olive with red, green, and orange tints.

Cirrhina sindensis, Day.

This species would not belong to the genus Cirhina, as defined by Günther. It is probably a Labeo.

HAB. Sind Hills. 8 inches.

CHAR. Barbels 2 ; maxillary, short. Dorsal rays 3 + 10. Anal 2 + 5. Scales 43, transverse 8 + 8. $6\frac{1}{2}$ rows between the lateral line and the ventral fin. Depth contained 4 times, head 4 times in the total. Eye situated in the middle of the length of the head. Mandibles sharp with a thin horny covering. Lips entire.

Cyprinus dero, H. B.

This fish may be a Labeo, but its true position is doubtful.

HAB. Bramapootra River. 4 inches.

CHAR. Barbels 2, small, maxillary. Mouth small, with a ridge on the lower jaw. The lateral line is below the middle and is bent downwards.

The colours of the back and belly are irregularly indented into each other on the sides.

Dorsal rays 13. Anal 7. Scales about 43 in the figure.

Chondrostoma gangeticum, Cuv.

Insufficiently described. This and the three following species are placed temporarily in the B. M. catalogue under the heading of Gymnostomus. They have no barbels.

HAB. Ganges.

CHAR. Dorsal rays 10. Anal 7. Scales 33.

Chondrostoma semivelatus, Cuv.

HAB. Madras.

CHAR. Dorsal rays 12. Anal 7. Scales 40.

Chondrostoma duvaucelli, Cuv.

HAB. Madras.

CHAR. Dorsal rays 11. Anal 7. Scales 40.

Chondrostoma fulungee, Sykes.

HAB. Deccan.

Cirrhina fulungee, Day.

Dr. Day describes a fish by this name, which he thinks is probably Sykes' fish.

HAB. Poona. 6 inches.

CHAR. Barbels 2, rostral. Dorsal rays 2 + 8. Anal 7. Scales 44, transverse 8 + 9. Depth contained 5 times, head 4 times in the total. 6½ rows between the lateral line and the ventrals.

Snout overhangs the mouth. Lips smooth.

Mayoa modesta, Day.

This species seems nearly to resemble *Discognathus macrochir*.

DESCRIPTION. "Mouth with an adhesive sucker

formed by both lips, and having a free margin, it is extended some distance posterior to the lower jaw as in the genus Discognathus, from which it essentially differs in that the sucker is completed by the upper lip, so as entirely to surround the opening of the mouth."

CHAR. Barbels 4. Scales 35. Dorsal rays 8. Anal 6. No scales on the chest.

A dark blotch under the dorsal fin, and a mark at the base of the caudal.

HAB. Probably Northern India. $3\frac{1}{2}$ inches.

Leuciscus rubripes, Jerdon.

This may be a Rasbora, or a Barilius. It was described from a single species and requires rediscovering.

HAB. Bowany River. · 6 inches.

DESCRIPTION. Dorsal rays 9. Anal 9. Scales 45, transverse 12. Barbels 2. Depth contained 4 times, head 4 times in total.

Mouth very slightly oblique. The dorsal arises above the interspace between the ventral and anal fins. Caudal fin lunate. Lateral lines bent downwards.

COLOURS: green above, golden on the sides, silvery beneath. Dorsal fin yellow, edged with black; pectorals yellow, ventral and anal white, tipped with vermilion, caudal pink in the centre, yellow externally.

Danio alburnus, Heckel.

HAB. Bombay.

This species is very insufficiently described, and there would seem to be no specimens extant. It appears to be very similar to *Danio osteographus*, (*Micronema*, B. M. catal.) but without markings on the side. Barbels apparently wanting.

Danio canarensis, Jerdon.

This again is a doubtful species.

HAB. Canara district.

CHAR. Dorsal rays 15. Anal 20,

Depth contained $2\frac{1}{2}$ times, head $4\frac{1}{4}$ times in the total.

Sides with blueish streaks. Barbels? Dr. Day considers it to be a female specimen of *Danio osteographus.*

Danio æquipinnatus, M'Clelland.

Apparently very similar to *Danio Nilgherriensis.*

M'Clelland calls it a very well-marked species.

HAB. Assam.

CHAR. Dorsal rays 13. Anal 13. Scales 32. 8 rows of scales from the back to the ventrals. Barbels none?

The depth of the body is from one-third to one quarter of the total length.

Danio æquipinnatus, Day.

This seems to be quite a distinct species; from the base of the Garo Hills, with the following characteristics.

Barbels 4, the rostral pair extending to the middle of the orbit.

Dorsal rays 12. Anal 14 to 16. Scales 32 to 34.

Several horizontal blue bars.

Similiogaster belangerii.

There seems to be no specimen of this fish in the British Museum. Valenciennes considered it as belonging to a genus distinct from Osteobrama, but Dr. Day seems to think that it must be identical with *Osteobrama microlepis*.

HAB. Bengal.

Abdomen sharp, without serrature.

CHAR. Dorsal rays 10. Anal 21. Scales 75, transverse 45.

Chela diffusa, Jerdon.

A species described by Dr. Jerdon from the Cavery River. Dr. Day suspects that it is the same as *Chela argentea*, in which case the latter name would have to be suppressed.

There appear to be no specimens in the British Museum of Jerdon's fish.

CHAR. Dorsal rays 9. Anal 17. Scales 50, transverse 9 or 10.

Profile of back perfectly straight. Length 4 to 6 inches.

Callichrous gangeticus, Peters.

In the B. M. Catal. this species is placed in the genus Cryptopterus. It is said to have come from the

Ganges, but has not been met with since it was described by Peters in 1861.

Body very long and narrow, the height being contained 9½ times, the length of the head nearly seven times in the total length (including the caudal fin).

Dorsal rays 2. Anal 75.

Haplochilus cyanophthalmus, Blyth.

HAB. Calcutta. 1¼ inches.

CHAR. Dorsal rays 7. Anal 22 or 23.

Colour whitish dotted with darker. Irides light blue.

Nandus marginatus, Jerdon.

HAB. Western Ghats, attaining 4 inches in length.

CHAR. Anal rays 11. Scales 25. Pseudobranchiæ present.

Trichogaster lalius, Buchanan.

In the B. M. Catalogue this is included as the same species as *Trichogaster fasciatus.* Dr. Day considers it distinct.

HAB. Rivers Jumna and Ganges. 2 inches.

CHAR. Dorsal fin rays 24, of which 16 are spinous. Anal fin rays 33, of which 18 are spinous.

Colour green with transverse red bars.

No lateral line. Head unarmed.

CHAPTER VI.

In this chapter I propose to collect a few facts of a miscellaneous character, from various sources, regarding Indian fishes, their habits, breeding, etc. There is not much reliable information to be had on these points, as observation is from the nature of the case difficult, and those who take a sufficient interest in the subject to devote their time to careful and patient investigation are few and far between.

First as regards their habits; in the cold months the generality of Indian fishes seem to lead a dormant and inactive existence, at least this is the case in Upper India. The rivers at this time are low, and the fish seem to resort to the deeper pools, where they lie quiescent at the bottom, neither seeming to care to move about, nor to feed; indeed those species that are naturally obliged to come to the surface to breathe at other times of the year, seem at this period able to exist without even a supply of fresh air.

Often, in places where rivers or streams issue from the hilly country into the plains, large, deep, and clear pools of water are to be found, sometimes running for long distances into the hills overshadowed by precipitous cliffs. In places of this sort the Mahaseer, Kalabans, and other large Cyprinoids may be seen in thousands lying near the bottom during the months of December, January, and February. In the Ganges above Hurdwar, for instance, where the water is brilliantly clear, although the stream is swift, I have seen, on looking over the side of a boat, thousands upon thousands of large fish crowded together.

I fancy the fact is that food is scarce at this time of year, the water weeds and vegetation die off and become rotten, and there are no insects or small fry about for the larger fish to feed upon. It is thus a necessity of their existence that at this time of year they should lie quiet and lead a semi-torpid kind of life, without caring to feed much, or to exert themselves by moving about, which would only increase their appetites.

In some parts of the country, where tanks abound which are apt to dry up altogether, several kinds of fish bury themselves in the mud, and are often dug out alive from thence by the natives. This fact, extraordinary as it may appear, has been so well attested by several observers as to leave no doubt of its actual truth. In this way it happens that on the first fall of rain full-grown fish are sometimes to be found in places that were a day or two previous hard and dry.

Some species, as the Anabas scandens and the Ophiocephalidæ, are able to travel a considerable distance on dry land; this they do when they find the water failing them in their own pond. They generally make their migrations during the night, and seem to possess an instinctive knowledge of the direction in which to proceed in order to reach water. They have often, however, been noticed travelling in the broad daylight, but this is a dangerous proceeding, as the kites and crows make short work of these fish out of water.

On the approach of spring the fish generally appear to wake up again. Their seasons are, however, much dependent upon the rains, which commence at different times in various parts of the country; thus in Assam the first rains fall in March, in the Punjab not until July.

Another cause that affects the streams of the Himalayan ranges is the melting of the snows, by which such of the rivers as have their sources among the higher hills are filled with cold snow-water during the first half of the year. Thus the habits of the fish vary in different rivers. As far as the Mahaseer are concerned, however, I believe that, generally speaking, March and April are considered the best months for fishing. When the rains begin, these fish commence moving up the streams for spawning purposes. At this time of year every rivulet becomes full, and places that were only dry boulder-strewn courses become full-grown streams. The Mahaseer, and many other Cyprinoid fish, are said not to deposit their spawn all at once like the salmon, but in several batches during a period of several months, say from May to August. In consequence they are never out of season or unfit for food, and may be taken all the year round. (In many species the interior is found to contain a copious oily secretion when breeding; this is not, I believe, the case with the Mahaseer.)

The time that they are in the best condition, fattest and most active, is at the commencement of the rains before they begin spawning, but their flesh will be found good and wholesome even in August, while by October they have quite recovered themselves again.

Thus, there is no necessity, in order to encourage the breeding of the Mahaseer in India, to place any restrictions on the capture of fish at certain seasons of the year, such as they are obliged to have in salmon-fisheries at home. Neither for other kinds of fish does it appear necessary, as the great majority, including all the kinds of most importance in an economical point of view, inhabit ponds and still waters in the plains, where they breed, and do not ascend to deposit their spawn into the small hill streams where they could be destroyed in a wholesale manner. The precautions necessary in this country are of a different description.

Nor yet in the case of the Mahaseer is it necessary

to provide for a clear passage for fish up the rivers, except in one or two special cases, for this reason; in the first burst of the rains, when the fish have to go up stream, the rivers are generally so much swollen that they have no difficulty whatever in reaching their destination. All impediments, excepting masonry irrigation works, which are not often met with, are cleared out of the way by the great rush of water.

It is after the rains are over, when the rivers are low again and the young fry are coming down stream, that care has to be taken of them. Often every drop of the water is strained through wicker-work traps, and the young fish are destroyed by millions.

It may, perhaps, be said that the fecundity of nature is so great that this destruction of fry does not perceptibly decrease the supply of fish.

To some degree this is no doubt true, but it should be remembered that the small fry are the natural food of many of the larger kinds, and if the former are destroyed by man, he cannot expect to find a plentiful supply of large fish as well, nor to have them in good condition and well fed. There is no doubt, I think, that when fish of any kind have an insufficient supply of food they never attain their full size, nor, I should imagine, that such kinds as naturally prefer a carnivorous diet, if forced to feed on vegetable matter, or filthy refuse, are not nearly so good or wholesome for eating. This consideration also disposes of the argument that, of the small fry taken in these basket-work traps, a large proportion are of species that would never attain a large size, or be of any importance as food.

To sum up, it seems that the fish supply of any district or river system is limited.

First, by the amount of water available for the fish during the winter, when the rivers are at their lowest.

Secondly, by the supply of food available for the fish. Some kinds, as the Siluroids and Ophiocephalidæ, are chiefly carnivorous; others, as the Cyprinidæ, feed on both vegetable and animal food. The former are mainly dependent for food on the smaller species which swarm in great profusion everywhere, or on the young fry of their own and other species or on frogs. The latter live chiefly on water-weeds and other vegetables, and consume also a vast quantity of water-snails and insects.

Thirdly, the supply of fish may be checked at the fountain-head by artificial interference with the conditions necessary to their reproduction, owing to the ignorance, cupidity, or apathy of the people of the country or their rulers.

Perhaps the most mischievous habit in this respect is the custom of poisoning streams which prevails in many hill districts. By this means every fish, large or small, in the water is destroyed, and it may be years before the fish supply in that stream can recover itself.

It would be a mistake, however, to condemn even

this practice in every instance without inquiry. In some cases fish poisoning may be carried on without bad effects, but it depends entirely on the character of the locality, and the process has to be conducted carefully. At the base of the Khasia Hills, for instance, towards Sylhet, the streams form pools, long, narrow, and very deep, which are full of splendid fish. The Khasias poison these pools on certain occasions, once, I think, in three years, and capture an enormous quantity of fish which they dry in the sun and which forms their principal diet till the next time comes round again. In this instance the harm done is not great, although it takes several years for the water to recover its supply of fish; but there is no other way in which the fish could be captured in this place, as nets could not be used, on account of the depth of the water, and the jagged limestone rocks. Neither are the fish wasted, but, on the contrary, being carefully dried, they form an important portion of the food supply of the adjoining villages. Also it is important to notice in this case that there is free water communication both with the upper portions of the streams and with the river below, from both of which sources these pools can become restocked. In other cases these conditions are not fulfilled, for example in these same Khasia Hills, in the streams on the plateau above, the natives seem to have practised the same method of capture that they find successful in the pools below, but here there are no means of naturally restocking these streams, and consequently there are now hardly any kinds of fish to be found at all in them. That this is not a natural condition seems probable. At one place I remember a tank about which the natives had a superstition, and in this there were numerous fish, but they considered it haunted, and never dared to destroy the fish, for fear of offending the ghost or demon who lived there.

Thus river poisoning may in certain cases be allowable, but only then under proper restrictions, while as a general rule it ought to be strictly forbidden.

The taking of small fry in basket-work traps should always be jealously guarded. It is a wasteful and improvident system, and although it might perhaps be permitted to a certain extent in certain places, so long as provision was made for a fair proportion of the little fish to make their way down stream, yet in most cases it would seem that if the practice could altogether be put a stop to there would result a great improvement in the quantity and the quality of the food supply. In deciding upon the necessity of any restrictive measures in any particular district, the question would resolve itself into this. Do the number of the fish destroyed in this manner form an appreciable proportion of the total supply of the district? If they do, measures are decidedly necessary for their protection.

In some parts of the country when the rains are over, the streams are entirely diverted from their proper courses, in order to irrigate the fields of rice and other crops.

Here the young fish thrive splendidly, but in each field where the water runs off, these traps are fixed. In consequence, hardly any of the fry can possibly ever reach the river again!

I need not further pursue this subject, as it is being investigated and reported upon by Dr. Day, Inspector General of Fisheries.

The Cyprinidæ are very prolific; they deposit a great number of eggs, apparently at intervals during the rainy season. The Siluridæ deposit fewer eggs, and of a large size; in some species of the genus Arius, the male fish is said to carry the eggs about in his mouth until they are hatched.

The Ophiocephalidæ are said to pair, living together in holes; the young remain with them a certain time in a shoal, being afterwards driven away by their parents to fish for themselves, or, if not inclined to be off quickly, are eaten up and disposed of by the affectionate old couple.

Many of the Indian species are unable to live entirely under the surface of the water, but have to come to the top every now and then to take in a supply of air. The Labyrinthici and the Ophiocephalidæ have an accessory chamber connected with the gills which enables them to breath the pure air. Thus they are able to live for days without water, or with only a little damp grass or mud. They have to pay however for this advantage, for if they are kept under water and prevented from reaching the surface, they quickly become drowned, especially if they are excited and moving much about. When remaining quiet, they seem to be able to keep under the surface a long time; perhaps at such times their gills are able to supply them with sufficient oxygen from the water, but when active they are obliged to come constantly to the surface.

Many kinds of fish do well in tanks, and will grow to a large size.

The species best adapted for this purpose seem to be the Roho, "Labeo Rohita," "Catla buchanani," "Cirrhina mrigala," "Barbus sarana," and some others. The Murrul, "Ophiocephalus marulius," grows to a large size, but it is a predaceous fish and will not get on with the other kinds. The same may be said of the large siluroids.

In stocking a pond, it is said to be the best plan to keep in it one species only, selecting a species that will grow to a large size. The Catla is perhaps the best for this purpose, as it is quick of growth and of first-rate quality as food. Besides this, there may be other fish of small kinds, but care should be taken to exclude all carnivorous species.

It should not be forgotten, however, that continuous interbreeding among the same stock is injurious. In old fish ponds it often happens that the fish get diseased from this cause, hence care should be taken to introduce fresh stock occasionally from a different locality.

As a rule it would seem advisable to employ for stocking ponds such species as naturally thrive best in the same part of the country, as these are more likely to succeed than species imported from other districts. It is not easy to tell beforehand what conditions are necessary for any particular species to live and breed, and especially to thrive, as they may be able just to exist without attaining the size or quality that they would do in their natural location. In places where particular species do not occur naturally, it would seem probable that the conditions are not favourable to them, unless any special reason is apparent for their non-appearance.

We are led to this inference by finding so many species in places that happen to be suited to them all over the Indian continent, though not to be found in intermediate localities, and also by the paucity of cases in which any species is confined only to one river-system or district.

I am alluding here only to Indian species. There might be among the Himalayan ranges many streams admirably adapted to European fish, such as trout, but no one would expect to find them there for this reason only. But if it were an Indian fish in question, I should say that the fact of any particular species not being found in a stream would be a good *primâ-facie* reason for concluding that the stream was not adapted to the requirements of that species, and that even if it were introduced from elsewhere it would not get on well therein.

These notes are necessarily very imperfect; they will suffice, however, to show what a large field for investigation lies open; and if one or two of my readers are hereby induced to turn their attention to this branch of inquiry, and to publish the results of their investigation, the object of this little work will have been attained.

ADDENDA.

The following four species are doubtful ones that should have been noticed in the Appendix to Chap. V.

Ophiocephalus nigricans, Cuvier.

This fish is said to come from the East Indies, but the locality seems doubtful.

DESCRIPTION. Dorsal rays 50. Anal 34. Large teeth in the lower jaw, on the vomer and palatine bones. Depth of body contained 9 times, length of head 4½ times in the total length.

COLOUR brownish black, with some indistinct darker bands across the back. Dorsal and caudal fins black.

Rita rama, Ham. Buchanan.

This small fish, found by Buchanan in the Bramaputra river, was described and figured by him under the name of *Pimelodus rama.* It would appear to belong to the Genus *Rita*, and may perhaps be the young of some larger species.

DESCRIPTION. Dorsal rays 8? Anal 15. Barbels 6, thick and shorter than the head.

COLOUR yellowish, body diaphanous. On the nape is a large black spot, divided into four lobes.

Danio chrysops, Cuvier.

Known only from Cuvier's description.

Scales 45. Dorsal rays 13. Anal 20.

Colour silvery.

Hab. Bengal.

Nemachilus guttatus, M'Clelland.

Said by M'Clelland to have only four barbels.

Hab. Tanks near Joorhath, in Upper Assam.

Colour light green with dark blotches. Dorsal rays 8.

LIST OF THE FRESH-WATER FISHES OF THE INDIAN CONTINENT.

NOT INCLUDING BURMAH OR CEYLON, AND EXCLUDING THOSE SPECIES THAT ARE PROPERLY MARINE.

Arranged according to the order observed in the Catalogue of the British Museum.

(NAMES IN ITALICS ARE THOSE OF DOUBTFUL SPECIES.)

	Reference to Günther's Catalogue.	Reference to the pages of the present volume.
PERCIDÆ.		
Ambassis nalua, H. B.	vol. i., p. 225	165
„ nama, H. B.	p. 228	166
„ ranga, H. B.	p. 228	165
„ lala, H. B.	p. 222	166
„ baculis, H. B. . . .	p. 222	166
„ thomassi, D.		166
GOBIIDÆ.		
Gobius giuris, H. B.	vol. iii., p. 21	167
„ malabaricus, D.		167
Euctenogobius striatus, D. . .		168
NANDIDÆ.		
Badis buchanani, Bkr.	vol. iii., p. 367	169
„ dario, H. B.	p. 367	169
Nandus marmoratus, Cuv. . . .	p. 367	170
„ *marginatus, J.*		191

	Reference to Günther's Catalogue.	Reference to the pages of the present volume.
LABYRINTHICI.		
Anabas scandens, Dald.	vol. iii., p. 375	171
Polyacanthus cupanus, Cuv.	p. 381	172
Osphromenus nobilis, M'C.	p. 384	172
Trichogaster fasciatus, Bloch.	p. 387	173
„ *lalius, H. B.*	p. 387	191
„ chuna, H. B.	p. 387	173
MUGILIDÆ.		
Mugil nepalensis, G.	vol. iii., p. 424	174
„ parsia, H. B.	p. 426	174
„ cantoris, Bkr.	p. 430	174
„ corsula, H. B.	p. 460	175
„ cascasia, H. B.	p. 410	175
OPHIOCEPHALIDÆ.		
Ophiocephalus punctatus, Bloch.	vol. iii., p. 469	176
„ gachua, H. B.	p. 471	176
„ striatus, Bloch.	p. 474	177
„ barca, H. B.	p. 477	177
„ nigricans, Cuv.	p. 477	
„ marulius, H. B.	p. 478	177
„ pseudomarulius, G.	p. 478	178
„ stewartii, Pl.		177
„ diplogramme, D.		178
MASTACEMBELIDÆ.		
Rhynchobdella aculeata, Bloch.	vol. iii., p. 540	179
Mastacemblus pancalus, H. B.	p. 541	179
„ armatus, Lacép.	p. 542	180
„ allepensis, Bloch.	p. 541	180
„ guentheri, D.		180
CHROMIDES.		
Eutroplus suratensis, Bloch.	vol. iv., p. 266	181
„ maculatus, Bloch.	p. 266	181

	Reference to Günther's Catalogue.	Reference to the pages of the present volume.
SILURIDÆ.		
Clarias magur, H. B.	vol. v., p. 17	124
„ jagur, H. B.	p. 21	124
Plotosus canius, H. B.	p. 25	125
„ limbatus, Cuv.	p. 25	125
Chaca lophioides, Cuv.	p. 29	125
„ buchanani, G.	p. 29	126
„ bankanensis, Bkr.	p. 29	126
Saccobranchus fossilis, Bloch. .	p. 31	126
Silurus cochinchinensis, Cuv. . .	p. 34	127
„ malabaricus, Cuv.	p. 34	127
„ dukai, D.		127
„ wynaadensis, D.		127
Silurichthys lamghur, H.	p. 36	128
Wallago attu, Bloch.	p. 36	128
Eutropiichthys vacha, H. B. . .	p. 38	131
Callichrous *gangeticus*, *Peters*. .	p. 44	190
„ bimaculatus, Bloch. .	p. 45	129
„ chechra, H. B. . . .	p. 46	129
„ pabda, H. B.	p. 47	130
„ anastomus, Cuv. . .	p. 47	130
„ canio, H. B.	p. 48	130
„ pabo, H. B.	p. 48	130
„ latovittatus, Pl. . . .		130
„ egertonii, D.		131
Eutropius obtusirostris, G. . . .	p. 53	131
Ailia bengalensis, Gray	p. 56	134
„ affinis, G.	p. 56	135
Ailiichthys punctata, D.		135
Schilbichthys garua, H. B. . . .	p. 57	134
Pseudeutropius murius, H. B. . .	p. 54	133
„ athernioides, Blch.	p. 58	132
„ mitchelli, G. . .	p. 59	132
„ megalops, G. . .	p. 60	133
„ longimanus, G. .	p. 60	133
„ goongwaree, S. .	p. 61	133
„ taakree, S. . .		133
„ sykesii, J. . . .		133

	Reference to Günther's Catalogue.	Reference to the pages of the present volume.
Pangasius buchanani, Cuv. . .	vol. v., p. 62	135
Silondia gangetica, Cuv. . . .	p. 65	136
Macrones cavasius, H. B. . . .	p. 76	137
,, aor, H. B.	p. 78	136
,, lamarrii, Cuv. . . .	p. 79	137
,, gulio, H. B.	p. 79	137
,, tengara, H. B. . . .	p. 81	137
,, carcio		138
,, batasio, H. B. . . .	p. 83	138
,, tengana, H. B. . . .	p. 84	138
,, keletius, Cuv. . . .	p. 84	138
,, chryseus, D.		139
,, corsula, H. B. . . .	p. 74	139
,, punctatus, J.		139
,, nangra, H. B. . . .		139
,, botius, H. B.		139
,, vittatus, Bloch . . .	p. 75	140
,, malabaricus, D. . . .		140
,, oculatus, Cuv. . . .		140
,, cavia, H. B.		140
Rita crucigera, Ow.	p. 92	141
,, pavimentata, V.	p. 93	141
,, hastata, V.	p. 93	141
,, kuturnee, S.	p. 93	142
,, ritoides, Cuv.		141
,, rama, H. B.	p. 92	
Olyra longicaudata, M'C. . . .	p. 98	142
,, laticeps, M'C.	p. 98	142
Arius gagorides, Cuv.	p. 140	143
,, arioides, Cuv.	p. 143	143
,, sona, H. B.		143
,, gagora, H. B.	p. 168	143
Hemipimelodus peronii, Cuv. . .	p. 177	144
,, viridescens, H. B.		144
Osteogeniosus militaris, L. . . .	p. 181	144
Batrachocephalus mino, H. B. . .	p. 182	145
Bagarius yarrellii, S.	p. 183	145
Glyptosternum trilineatum, Bly. .	p. 185	146
,, gracile, G. . . .	p. 186	146

	Reference to Günther's Catalogue.	Reference to the pages of the present volume.
Glyptosternum lonah, S.	vol. v., p. 187	147
„ dekkanense, G. . .	p. 187	147
„ striatum, M'C. . .	p. 188	147
„ pectinopterum, M'C.	p. 188	147
„ telchitta, H. B. .	p. 185	148
„ modestum, D. . .		148
Amblyceps tenuispinis, Bly. . .	p. 190	148
„ mangois, H. B.	p. 190	149
Callomystax gagata, H. B.	p. 218	149
Sisor rhabdophorus, H. B. . . .	p. 262	150
Erethistes pusillus, M.	p. 264	151
„ hara, H. B. (Hara buchanani, Günth.) . .	p. 189	151
„ conta, H. B. (Hara conta, Günth.)	p. 189	151
„ jerdoni, D.		151
„ elongata, D.		151
Pseudecheneis sulcatus, M'C. . .	p. 264	152
Exostoma labiatum, M'C. . . .	p. 265	152
„ blythii, D.		152
SCOMBRESOCIDÆ.		
Belone cancila, H. B.	vol. vi., p.	153
Hemiramphus ectuntio, H. B. .		154
„ brachynotopterus, Bkr.		154
CYPRINODONTIDÆ.		
Haplochilus panchax, H. B. . .		155
„ cyanophthalmus, Bly.		191
„ lineatus, Cuv. . . .		156
„ melastigmas, M'C. .		156
„ argenteus, D. . . .		156
„ rubrostigmus, J. . .		156
Cyprinodon stolickanus, D. . . .		155
CYPRINIDÆ.		
Catla buchanani, Cuv.	vol. vii. p. 34	80

	Reference to Günther's Catalogue.	Reference to the pages of the present volume.
Cirrhina mrigala, H. B.	vol. vii., p. 35	67
„ leschenaultii, Cuv. . . .	p. 36	67
„ anisura, M'C.	p. 37	67
„ dyochilus, M'C.	p. 37	68
„ sindensis, D.		186
„ dero, H. B.		186
„ bata, H. B.	p. 35	68
„ fulungee, D.		187
Labeo nandina, H. B.	p. 51	61
„ fimbriatus, Bloch.	p. 53	61
„ leschenaultii, Cuv.	p. 53	185
„ calbasu, H. B.	p. 54	62
„ porcellus, H.	p. 54	62
„ rohita, H. B.	p. 55	63
„ kontius, J.	p. 55	64
„ morala, H. B.	p. 56	64
„ diplostomus, H.	p. 57	65
„ ricnorhynchus, M'C. . . .	p. 57	64
„ falcatus, Gray.	p. 58	64
„ pangusia, H. B.	p. 58	65
„ dussumieri, Cuv.	p. 59	63
„ gonius, H. B.	p. 59	63
„ cursa, H. B.	p. 60	63
„ nancar, H. B.	p. 25	185
„ nigrescens, D.		62
„ nashii, D.		66
„ striolatus, G.	p. 62	66
„ ariza, H. B.	p. 63	65
„ boga, H. B.	p. 64	65
„ boggut, S.	p. 35	185
„ bicolor, M'C.	p. 76	65
„ mullya, S.	p. 76	186
„ nukta, S.	p. 32	65
Mayoa modesta, D.		187
Discognathus lamta, H. B.	p. 69	73
„ macrochir, G. . . .	p. 70	73
Crossochilus latius, H. B.	p. 71	69
„ gohama, H. B. . . .	p. 72	69
„ rostratus, G.	p. 72	70

	Reference to Günther's Catalogue.	Reference to the pages of the present volume.
Crossochilus barbatulus, H. . . .	vol. vii., p. 72	70
„ sada, H. B.	p. 74	70
„ reba, H. B.	p. 74	70
„ mosario, H. B. . . .	p. 71	71
„ isurus, M'C.	p. 63	71
Gymnostomus gangeticum, Cuv. .	p. 76	187
„ *semivelatus, Cuv.* .	p. 76	187
„ *duvaucellii, Cuv.* . .	p. 76	187
„ *fulungee, S.*	p. 76	187
Capöeta watsoni, D.		79
„ irregularis, D.		79
Barbus spilopholis, M'C. . . .	p. 96	46
„ chagunio, H. B. (beavani, Gunth.)	p. 96	47
„ clavatus, M'C.	p. 97	47
„ immaculatus, M'C.	p. 113	48
„ *chrysopoma, Cuv.*	p. 113	182
„ pinnauratus, D.	p. 114	48
„ sarana, H. B.	p. 115	47
„ *russellii, G.*	p. 121	182
„ *polydori, Cuv.*	p. 122	183
„ micropogon, Cuv.	p. 126	45
„ conirostris, G.	p. 127	44
„ dubius, D.	p. 127	45
„ chilinoides, M'C.	p. 127	44
„ carnaticus, J.	p. 128	44
„ spinulosus, M'C.	p. 128	48
„ hexastichus, M'C.	p. 129	44
„ mosal, H. B.	p. 130	41
„ melanampyx, D. (arulius, G.)	p. 133	49
„ roseipinnis, Cuv.	p. 83	48
„ jerdoni, D.		46
„ sophore, H. B. (not Günth.)		45
„ neilli, D.		45
„ compressus, D.		45
„ himalayanus, D.		44
„ pulchellus, D.		48
„ thomassi, D.		49
„ lithopodos, D.		49

	Reference to Günther's Catalogue.	Reference to the pages of the present volume.
Barbus kolus, S.	vol. vii., p. 136	52
" *liacanthus, Bkr.*	p. 141	183
" dorsalis, J.	p. 142	50
" thermalis, Cuv.	p. 143	50
" chola, H. B.	p. 143	50
" *sophoroides, G.*	p. 144	183
" amphibius, Cuv.	p. 144	50
" titius, H. B.	.	51
" lepidus, D. (filamentosus, G. cat.)	p. 145	51
" denisonii, D.	p. 146	52
" *hamiltonii, D.*	p. 146	184
" parrah, D.		51
" curmuca, H. B.	p. 83	52
" arulius, J. (not Günth.)		52
" puckelli, D.		53
" duvaucelii, Cuv.	p. 151	56
" stigma, Cuv. (sophore, Günth. cat.)	p. 152	56
" chrysopterus, M'C.	p. 152	57
" ticto, H. B.	p. 153	54
" conchonius, H. B.	p. 153	55
" terio, H. B.	p. 153	57
" puntio, H. B.	p. 154	59
" tetrarupagus, M'C. (titius, Günth. cat.)	p. 154	58
" phutonio, H. B.	p. 154	55
" gelius, H. B.	p. 154	55
" vittatus, D.	p. 156	58
" modestus, Kner.	p. 156	57
" cosuatis, H. B.	p. 157	59
" pyrrhopterus, M'C.	p. 157	56
" ambassis, D.		54
" punctatus, D.		56
" guganio, H. B.	p. 83	56
" filamentosus, Cuv. (not Günth.)		58
" waageni, D.		59
" *presbyter, Cuv.*		184

	Reference to Günther's Catalogue.	Reference to the pages of the present volume.
Barbus punjabensis, D.		59
Oreinus micracanthus, G. . . .	vol. vii., p. 81	76
„ plagiostomus, H.	p. 160	75
„ sinuatus, H.	p. 161	76
„ richardsonii, Gray. . . .	p. 161	76
„ *progastus, M'C.*	p. 160	184
Schizothorax planifrons, H. . .	p. 163	77
„ micropogon, H. . . .	p. 163	77
„ hugelii, H. . . .	p. 164	77
„ curvifrons, H. . . .	p. 164	77
„ niger, H.	p. 164	77
„ nasus, H.	p. 166	78
„ longipinnis, H. . . .	p. 166	78
„ esocinus, H. . . .	p. 166	78
„ hodgsonii, G. . . .	p. 167	79
„ nobilis, M'C. . . .	p. 162	78
„ gobioides, M'C. . .	p. 162	78
Rasbora daniconius, H. B. . . .	p. 194	81
„ buchanani, Bkr. . . .	p. 196	81
„ neilgherriensis, D. . .	p. 197	81
„ elanga, H. B.	p. 198	81
Nuria danrica, H. B.	p. 200	82
„ malabarica, D.	p. 200	82
Amblypharyngodon mola, H. B. .	p. 202	83
„ pellucidus, M'C.	p. 202	83
„ melettinus, Cuv.	p. 202	83
Thynnichthys harengula, Cuv. .	p. 157	84
Semiplotus M'Clellandi, Bkr. . .	p. 204	84
„ brevidorsalis, D. . .		85
Danio dangila, H. B.	p. 282	86
„ lineolatus, Bly.	p. 282	86
„ osteographus, M'C. (micronema, Günth. cat.) . .	p. 282	86
„ *alburnus, H.*	p. 283	189
„ aurolineatus, D. (malabaricus, Günth. cat.) . . .	p. 283	87
„ neilgherriensis, D.	p. 283	87
„ *canarensis, J.*	p. 284	189
„ devario, H. B.	p. 284	88

	Reference to Günther's Catalogue.	Reference to the pages of the present volume.
Danio *chrysops, Cuv.*	vol. vii., p. 281	
„ æquipinnatus, M'C.	p. 285	189
„ æquipinnatus, D.		189
Pteropsarion bakeri, D.	p. 284	88
Aspidoparia morar, H. B. . . .	p. 285	95
„ sardina, H.	p. 285	95
„ jaya, H. B.	p. 286	96
Barilius tileo, H. B.	p. 287	93
„ radiolatus, G.	p. 287	89
„ bendelesis, H. B.	p. 288	90
„ cocsa, H. B.	p. 288	90
„ alburnus, G.	p. 289	90
„ morarensis, G.	p. 290	91
„ bicirratus, M'C.	p. 290	91
„ modestus, D.		91
„ barna, H. B.	p. 290	92
„ barila, H. B.	p. 291	92
„ gatensis, Cuv.	p. 291	92
„ rerio, H. B.	p. 292	89
„ bleekeri, D.		91
„ vagra, H. B.	p. 286	92
„ canarensis, J.	p. 284	93
„ papillatus, D.		93
„ borelio, H. B.	p. 286	93
„ evezardi, D.		94
Bola goha, H. B.	p. 293	94
Schacra cirrhata, M'C.	p. 294	95
Osteobrama cotio, H. B.	p. 323	96
„ rapax, G.	p. 323	97
„ alfrediana, Cuv. . . .	p. 324	97
„ ogilbii, S.	p. 324	98
„ microlepis, Bly. . .	p. 325	98
„ neilli, D.		98
„ bakeri, D.		99
Similiogaster belangerii, Cuv. . . .	p. 328	190
Chela gora, H. B.	p. 332	100
„ bacaila, H. B.	p. 332	100
„ clupeoides, Bloch.	p. 333	101
„ phulo, H. B.	p. 334	100

	Reference to Günther's Catalogue.	Reference to the pages of the present volume.
Chela novacula, Val.	vol. vii., p. 334	101
„ *diffusa, J.*	p. 334	190
„ argentea, D.	p. 334	102
„ laubuca, H. B.	p. 335	103
„ perseus, M'C.	p. 331	103
„ untrahi, D.		101 .
„ flavipinnis, J.	p. 334	101
„ punjabensis, D.		100
„ boopis, D.		102
Cachius atpar, H. B.	p. 339	104
Homaloptera maculata, Gray . .	p. 340	104
„ brucei, Gray . . .	p. 340	105
Psilorhynchus sucatio, H. B. . .	p. 343	74
„ balitora, H. B. . .	p. 343	74
Misgurnus lateralis, G.	p. 346	106
Nemachilus pavonaceus, M'C. .	p. 348	106
„ botia, H. B.	p. 349	106
„ montanus, M'C. . . .	p. 350	107
„ beavani, G.	p. 350	107
„ rupecola, M'C.	p. 351	107
„ subfuscus, M'C. . . .	p. 351	108
„ denisonii, D.	p. 352	108
„ notostigma, Bkr. . .	p. 352	108
„ triangularis, D. . . .	p. 352	108
„ semiarmatus, D. . .	p. 353	107
„ striatus, D.	p. 353	108
„ savona, H. B. . . .	p. 354	109
„ marmoratus, H. . . .	p. 356	109
„ spilopterus, Cuv. . . .	p. 358	109
„ butanensis, M'C. . .	p. 358	109
„ monoceros, M'C. . .	p. 358	107
„ griffithii, G. . . .	p. 360	110
„ turio, H. B.	p. 360	110
„ corica, H. B.	p. 361	110
„ guentheri, D.	p. 361	110
„ phoxochilus, M'C. .	p. 361	110
„ *guttatus, M'C.*	p. 361	
„ rupelli, S.	p. 347	106
„ moreh, S.	p. 347	106

	Reference to Günther's Catalogue.	Reference to the pages of the present volume.
Nemachilus aureus, D.		107
„ zonatus, M'C.	vol. vii., p. 347	108
„ sinuatus, D.		108
„ chlorosoma, M'C.	p. 347	110
„ serpentarius, D.		110
„ mugah, D.		109
„ blythii, D.		110
„ rubripinnis, J.	p. 347	109
„ evezardi, D.		111
Cobitis guntea, H. B.	p. 363	111
„ gongota, H. B.	p. 363	111
Lepidocephalichthys thermalis, Cuv.	p. 364	112
„ balgara, H. B.	p. 365	112
Botia dario, H. B.	p. 366	112
„ almorhæ, Gray	p. 367	113
„ rostrata, G.	p. 367	113
„ nebulosa, Bly.	p. 366	113
„ berdmorei, Bly.	p. 366	113
Acanthophthalmus pangia, H. B.	p. 370	114
Jerdonia maculata, D.		113
CLUPEIDÆ.		
Engraulis purava, H. B.	vol. vii., p. 397	115
„ mystax, Bloch.	p. 397	116
„ taty, Cuv.	p. 400	116
„ telara, H. B.	p. 401	116
Clupeoides sorbona, H. B.		119
Chatoëssus cortius, H. B.	p. 410	117
„ chanpole, H. B.	p. 410	117
„ manmina, H. B.	p. 406	117
Clupea indica, Gray	p. 444	118
„ chapra, Gray	p. 447	118
Pellona motius, H. B.	p. 456	119
„ dussumieri, Cuv.	p. 457	119
Megalops cyprinoides, Brouss.	p. 471	120
NOTOPTERIDÆ.		
Notopterus chitala, H. B.	vol. vii., p. 479	121
„ kapirat, Lacép.	p. 480	122

	Reference to Günther's Catalogue.	Reference to the pages of the present volume.
SYMBRANCHIDÆ.		
Amphipnous cuchia, H. B.	vol. viii., p. 13	157
Symbranchus bengalensis, M'C. .	p. 16	158
MURÆNIDÆ.		
Anguilla bengalensis, Gray . . .	vol. viii., p. 27	159
„ bicolor, M'C.	p. 35	159
Ophichthys hyala, H. B. . . .	p. 60	159
Moringua raitaborua, H. B. . .	p. 90	160
SYNGNATHIDÆ.		
Doryichthys deocata, H. B. . .	vol. viii., p. 179	161
GYMNODONTES.		
Tetrodon patoca, H. B.	vol. viii., p. 288	162
„ cutcutia, H. B. . . .	p. 290	163
„ fluviatilis, H. B. . . .	p. 299	163

INDEX

TO NATIVE NAMES AND SYNONYMS.

Bidah	Sind.	Cachius atpar.
Bikree	Oudh.	Schilbichthys garua.
Bikuntia	Ooriah.	Macrones tengara.
Billi	Punj.	Amblyceps mangois.
Bilturi	Assam.	Nemachilus botia.
bilturio, Cobitis	H.B.	Nemachilus botia.
bimucromata, Cobitis	M'C.	Nemachilus botia.
bimaculatus, Cyprinus	H. B.	Barbus ticto.
bimaculatus, Gonorhynchus	M'C.	Discognathus lamta.
Bipotassi	Ooriah.	Pseudeutropius atherinoides.
birmannus, Bagrus	Cuv.	Macrones gulio.
Bitchu ke mutchlee	Hind.	Saccobranchus fossilis.
blochii, Cirrhina	Cuv.	Cirrhina leschenaultii.
blythii, Rohtee	Bkr.	Osteobrama microlepis.
Boahree	N. W. P.	Barbus chrysopterus.
boalis, Silurus	H. B.	Wallago attu.
boalis, Schilbe	S.	Wallago attu.
Boallee	Hind.	Wallago attu.
Boassa	Hind.	Catla buchanani.
bobree, Varicorhinus	S.	Labeo fimbriatus ?
Bodosi	Ooriah.	Nandus marmoratus.
boga, Cyprinus	H. B.	Labeo (Tylognathus) boga.
boggut, Chondrostoma	S.	Labeo boggut.
bogoda, Chanda	H. B.	Ambassis nama.
Bokar	Assam.	Barbus hexastichus.
bola, Barilius	D.	Bola goha.
bola, Cyprinus	H. B.	Bola goha.
Bommiday	Tel.	Rhynchobdella aculeata.
bontianus, Notopterus	Cuv.	Notopterus kapirat.
Bonkuaso	Ooriah.	Cachius atpar.
Boolla	Hind.	Labeo falcatus.
Boondei	Ooriah.	Badis buchanani.
Bopotassi	Ooriah.	Pseudeutropius atherinoides.
Bora	Bhutan.	Ophiocephalus barca.
Borajallee	Assam.	Barbus tetrarupagus.
Boreli	Beng.	Barilius borelio.
borelio, Cyprinus	H. B.	Barilius borelio.
Botchee	Tel.	Catla buchanani.
botia, Cobitis	H. B.	Nemachilus botia.
botius, Pimelodus	H. B.	Macrones botius.
Boul-la	Punj.	Gobius giuris.
Bounceputtri	Ooriah.	Ailia bengalensis.
Bounchee	Punj.	Chela gora.
bovianus, Gobio	J.	Labeo (Tylognathus) ariza.
brachialis, Opsarius	M'C.	Barilius tileo ?
brachiatus, Leuciscus	M'C.	Barilius cocsa.
brachypterus, Gonorhynchus	M'C.	Discognathus lamta.
branchiatus, Leuciscus	M'C.	Barilius cocsa.
brevifilis, Engraulis	Cuv.	Engraulis telara.
brevirostris, Anguilla	M'C.	Anguilla bengalensis.
brevis, Gonorhynchus	M'C.	Crossochilus gohama.
brevis, Ptyobranchus	M'C.	Moringua raitaborua.
brucei, Balitora	Gray.	Homaloptera brucei.
Buah	Punj.	Mugil cascasia.
buchanani, Bagarius	Bkr.	Bagarius yarellii.

Chinta-jellah	R.	Arius?
chinta, Bagrus	Cuv.	Arius?
Chippuah	Hind.	Aspidoparia morar.
Chiri	Punj.	Badis buchanani.
Chital	Punj.	Nemachilus rupecola.
chitala, Mystus	H. B.	Notopterus chitala.
Chitol	Beng.	Notopterus chitala.
Chitrahtoo	Punj.	Barbus himalayanus.
Chittahri	Tel.	Crossochilus reba.
chitul, Leuciscus	S.	? Amblypharyngodon melettinus.
chlorosoma, Cobitis	M'C.	Nemachilus chlorosomus.
Choaksi	Beng.	Discognathus lamta.
Choaree verarl	Mal.	Ophiocephalus marulius.
chola, Cyprinus	H. B.	Barbus chola.
Chola pungti	Beng.	Barbus chola.
Chola	Assam.	Aspidoparia jaya.
chola, Systomus	J.	Barbus hamiltonii?
Chota kukura	Beng.	Cobitis gongota.
Chota Saol	Punj.	Ophiocephalus striatus.
Chouldhi	Punj.	Nemachilus corica.
Chowloo-pamoo	R.	Anguilla bengalensis.
chrysopoma, Systomus	J.	Barbus chrysopoma.
chrysopoma, Puntius	D.	Barbus chrysopoma.
chrysops, Leuciscus	Cuv.	Danio chrysops.
chrysopterus, Systomus	M'C.	Barbus chrysopterus.
chrysosomus, Systomus	M'C.	Barbus immaculatus.
chrysostigmus, Aplocheilus	M'C.	Haplochilus panchax.
Chubboo	Punj.	Ophiocephalus gachua.
Chuchee	Sind.	Clupea indica.
Chula	Assam.	Aspidoparia morar.
chuna, Trichopodus	H. B.	Trichogaster chuna.
Chundra	Hind.	Ambassis ranga.
Churinga	Hind.	Ophiocephalus gachua.
Chutichi	Mal.	Nandus marginatus.
cinnamonea, Cobitis	M'C.	Acanthophthalmus pangia.
cinnamonea, Pangio	Bly.	Acanthophthalmus pangia.
cirratus, Opsarius	M'C.	Schacra cirrhata.
Cirreoh	Sind.	Labeo cursa.
cirrhosus, Cyprinus	Bloch.	Cirrhina leschenaultii.
clupeoides, Cyprinus	Bloch.	Chela clupeoides.
clupeoides, Leuciscus	Cuv.	Chela clupeoides.
Coal-ariza candee	Tamil.	Labeo ariza.
Coatee cundee	Tam.	Barbus conirostris.
cobojius, Coius	H. B.	Anabas scandens.
cocsa, Chedrus	Stein.	Barilius cocsa.
cocsa, Cyprinus	H. B.	Barilius cocsa.
Coi	Beng.	Anabas scandens.
coila, Malapterurus	H. B.	Ailia bengalensis.
Coilia	Ooriah.	Trichogaster fasciatus.
colisa, Trichopodus	H. B.	Trichogaster fasciatus.
conchonius, Cyprinus	H. B.	Barbus conchonius.
conchonius, Puntius	Stein.	Barbus conchonius.
conta, Pimelodus	H. B.	Erethistes conta.
Cooloosee	Hind.	Labeo cursa.

Name	Authority	Species
Coonchelie	N. W. P.	Chela laubuca.
Coondallum-ooloowaγ	Tamil.	Euctenogobius striatus.
Cooravoo	Mal.	Ophiocephalus marulius.
coramota, Ophiocephalus	Cuv.	Ophiocephalus gachua.
corica, Cobitis	H. B.	Nemachilus corica.
Corsula	Beng.	Mugil corsula.
corsula, Pimelodus	H. B.	Macrones corsula.
corsula, Bagrus	Cuv.	Macrones corsula.
cortius, Clupanodon	H. B.	Chatöessus cortius.
Corvu	Ooriah.	Anabas scandens.
cosuatis, Cyprinus	H. B.	Barbus cosuatis.
cosuatis, Leuciscus	Bkr.	Barbus cosuatis.
cotio, Cyprinus	H. B.	Osteobrama alfrediana.
cotio, Rohtee	D.	Osteobrama cotio.
cotis, Abramis	M'C.	Osteobrama cotio.
cotis, Osteobrama	Heckel.	Osteobrama cotio.
cotis, Osteobrama	Blyth.	Osteobrama alfrediana.
cotra, Colisa	Cuv	Trichogaster fasciatus.
cotra, Trichopodus	H. B.	Trichogaster fasciatus.
Courie	Assam.	Labeo cursa.
Coursa	Hind.	Labeo cursa.
Cowlie	Tamil.	Danio neilgherriensis.
crenulatus, Discognathus	Heckel.	Discognathus lamta.
cruciger, Arius	Owen.	Rita crucigera.
Cuaree	Mal.	Macrones oculatus.
cuchia, Symbranchus	D.	Amphipnous cuchia.
cuchia, Unibrancapertura	H. B.	Amphipnous cuchia.
Cucksee	Punj.	Mugil cascasia.
cucura, Cobitis	H. B.	Cobitis gongota.
culius, Cheilo-dipterus	H. B.	Eleotris fusca.
Cullah	Beng.	Mugil corsula.
cultellus, Leuciscus	Cuv.	Chela ?
cultellus, Pelecus	J.	Chela ?
Cumboo-kellettee	Tamil.	Macrones aor.
Cundah la	Ooriah.	Etroplus suratensis.
Cundalah	Sind.	Chela bacaila.
cundinga, Cyprinodon	H. B.	Megalops cyprinoides.
cundinga, Elops	Cant.	Megalops cyprinoides.
Cunnay	Mal.	Megalops cyprinoides.
cura, Cyprinus	H. B.	Cirrhina bata.
curchius, Cyprinus	H. B.	Labeo cursa.
curchius Labeo	D.	Labeo cursa.
curmuca, Cyprinus	H. B.	Barbus curmuca.
Curroo	Sind.	Crossochilus gohama.
Currummunnee-candee	Tamil.	Labeo kontius.
Currupoo-verarl	Tamil.	Ophiocephalus striatus.
cursa, Cyprinus	H. B.	Labeo cursa.
cursis, Cyprinus	H. B.	Labeo cursa.
Cursua	Ooriah.	Labeo cursa.
curtifilis, Megalops	Rich.	Megalops cyprinoides.
Cutta	Tamil.	Macrones cavasius.
Cuttapoh	Ooriah.	Barbus gelius.
Cutukhugger	Punj.	Macrones cavasius.
Cutwal alise	Ooriah.	Clupeoides soborna.
cuvieri, Cirrhinus	J.	Cirrhina leschenaultii.

cuvieri, Silurus	Gray.	Ailia bengalensis.
cyanophthalmus, Panchax .	Bly.	Haplochilus cyanophthalmus.
cyanotænia, Devario . . .	Bkr.	Danio osteographus.
cyprinoides, Clupea . . .	Brouss.	Megalops cyprinoides.
cyprinoides, Clupea . . .	Sch.	Chela clupeoides.
Dabah	N. W. P.	Danio devario.
Dahrah.	Punj.	Barilius cocsa.
Dahwiee	Hind.	Rasbora elanga.
dancena, Cyprinus	H. B.	Chela ?
dandia, Leuciscus	Cuv.	Rasbora daniconius.
dandia, Rasbora	Bkr.	
dangila, Cyprinus	H. B.	Danio dangila.
daniconius, Cyprinus . . .	H. B.	Rasbora daniconius.
daniconius, Leuciscus . . .	M'C.	Rasbora elanga.
daniconius, Opsarius . . .	Kner.	Rasbora daniconius.
Dankena	Beng.	Chela laubuca.
Dannahrah	Hind.	
danrica, Cyprinus	H. B.	Nuria danrica.
danrica, Esomus	Bkr.	
Dapeghat	Cashmere.	Schizothorax longipinnis.
dario, Cobitis.	H. B.	Botia dario.
dario, Labrus	H. B.	Badis dario.
Debari	Beng.	Danio devario.
deliciosus, Barbus	M'C.	Barbus immaculatus.
denisonii, Labeo	D.	Barbus denisonii.
denisonii, Puntius	D.	
deocata, Syngnathus . . .	H. B.	Doryichthys deocata.
dero, Cyprinus	H. B.	Labeo ? dero.
devario, Cyprinus	H. B.	Danio devario.
Dhengro	Assam.	Labeo ? dero.
Dheri dhok	Punj.	Ophiocephalus gachua.
Dhoguru	Punj.	Discognathus lamta.
Dhonga nu	Sind.	Schilbichthys garua.
Dhuggu	Sind.	Ophiocephalus punctatus.
Di, Dihee	Punj.	Labeo calbasu.
diffusus, Pelecus	J.	Chela diffusa.
Dimmon	Sind.	Callichrous chechra.
Dinnawah.	Hind.	Schizothorax hodgsonii.
diplochilus, Barbus . . .	Heck.	Crossochilus barbatulus.
diplochilus, Crossocheilus .	Stein.	
diplochilus, Cirrhina . . .	D.	Crossochilus barbatulus.
diplostomus, Varicorhinus .	Heck.	Labeo diplostomus.
Doarah.	Punj.	Ophiocephalus gachua.
Domarci batta	Beng.	Cirrhina bata.
Dondoo, Paum	R.	? Amphipnous cuchia.
Dongu	Cashmere.	Schizothorax nasus.
Doodhera	Beng.	Labeo ?
Doordah	Punj.	Barbus terio.
Doorkah	Punj.	Barbus chrysopterus.
Dorikana	Beng.	Amblypharyngodon pellucidus.
dorsalis, Systomus	J.	Barbus dorsalis.
dorsovittatus, Arothron . .	Bly.	Tetrodon fluviatilis.
Dowlah.	Punj.	Ophiocephalus marulius.
dualis, Opsarius.	J.	Barilius cocsa ?

Name	Authority	Species
dubius, Puntius	D.	Barbus dubius.
duda, Silurus	H. B.	Callichrous canio.
Dudha pabda	Beng.	Callichrous canio.
Duhrie	Punj.	Osteobrama cotio.
Duhrie	N. W. P.	Danio devario.
Dullounga	Punj.	Ophiocephalus punctatus.
Dumbrah	Sind.	Labeo rohita.
Dumsah	Punj.	Macrones tengana.
Dundikerri	Ooriah.	Rasbora daniconius.
Dungudah porah	Ooriah.	Cirrhina bata.
Dunnahree	Hind.	Chela phulo.
Durhie	Hind.	Barbus sarana.
Durmurua	Beng.	Gobius giuris.
Durru	Sind.	Barbus chrysopterus.
dussumieri, Ambassis	Cuv.	Ambassis nalua.
dussumieri, Cirrhina	Cuv.	Crossochilus reba.
dussumieri, Cirrhinichthys	Bkr.	Crossochilus reba.
dussumieri, Cirrhinus	J.	Labeo dussumieri.
dussumieri, Clarias	Cuv.	Clarias?
dussumieri, Leuciscus	Cuv.	Chela clupeoides.
dussumieri, Rohita	Cuv.	Labeo dussumieri.
dussumierii, Engraulis	Cuv.	Engraulis mystax.
duvaucelii, Barbus	Cuv.	Barbus immaculatus.
duvaucelii, Chondrostoma	Cuv.	Gymnostomus duvaucellii.
duvaucelii, Leuciscus	Cuv. p. 77.	Osteobrama alfrediana.
duvaucelii, Leuciscus	Cuv. p. 95.	Barbus duvaucelii.
duvaucelii, Systomus	Bkr.	Barbus duvaucelii.
duvaucellii, Rohita	Cuv.	? Labeo rohita.
dyangra, Cyprinus	M'C.	Crossochilus gohama.
dyocheilus, Catastomus / Cyprinus	M'C.	Cirrhina dyochilus.
dystomus, Leuciscus	M'C.	Rasbora elanga.
Ectuntio, Esox	H. B.	Hemiramphus ectuntio.
Eelemose	Tel.	Crossochilus reba.
einthovenii, Leuciscus / Rasbora	Bkr.	Rasbora daniconius.
elanga, Cyprinus	H. B.	Rasbora elanga.
elegans, Paradanio	D.	Cachius atpar.
elingulatus Leuciscus / Perilampus	M'C.	? Aspidoparia jaya.
elphinstonei, Anguilla	S.	Anguilla bengalensis.
erythreus, Ptyobranchus	M'C.	Moringua raitaborua.
exodon, Bagrus	Bkr.	Pseudeutropius atherinoides.
exodon, Bagrus	Cuv.	Pseudeutropius?
Falcata, Cyprinus	Gray.	Labeo falcatus.
fasciatus, Cirrhinus	J.	Labeo (Tylognathus)?
fasciatus, Opsarius	M'C.	Barilius barna.
fasciatus, Polyacanthus	Cuv.	Trichogaster fasciatus.
fascio-punctatus, Gobius	Rich.	Gobius giuris.
filamentosus, Barbus	Günth.	Barbus lepidus.
filamentosus, Megalops	Lacép.	Megalops cyprinoides.
filamentosus, Leuciscus	Cuv.	Barbus filamentosus.
filamentosus, Puntius	D.	Barbus filamentosus.
filamentosus, Systomus	J.	Barbus filamentosus.

Name	Authority	Synonym
fimbriata, Rohita	Cuv.	Labeo fimbriatus.
fimbriatus, Cyprinus	Bloch.	
fimbriatus, Gonorhynchus .	M'C.	Crossochilus sada.
fimbriatus, Labeo	Cuv.	Labeo rohita ?
flavipinnis, Pelecus	J.	Chela flavipinnis.
flavus, Leuciscus	J.	Rasbora buchanani.
fluviatilis, Crayracion . .	Bkr.	Tetrodon fluviatilis.
fossilis, Silurus	Bloch.	Saccobranchus fossilis.
fulungee, Chondrostoma . .	S.	Cirrhina fulungee.
fulvescens, Perilampus . .	Bly.	Chela, or Danio (?)
fuscus, Bagrus	Cuv.	Macrones gulio.
fuscus, Ophiocephalus . .	Cuv.	Ophiocephalus gachua.
fusiformis, Discognathus .	H.	Discognathus lamta.
fusiformis, Gobius	Bkr.	Gobius giuris.
Gagata, Pimelodus	H. B.	Callomystax gagata.
gagora, Arius	Cuv.	Arius gagora.
gagora, Pimelodus	H. B.	
gagorides, Bagrus	Cuv.	Arius gagorides.
Gaice	Beng.	Chela laubuca.
Gandumenoo	Tel.	Labeo fimbriatus.
gangeticum, Chondrostoma .	Cuv.	Gymnostomus gangeticus.
gangeticus, { Cryptopterus .	G.	Callichrous gangeticus.
gangeticus, { Pterocryptis .	Peters.	
garua, Silurus	H. B.	Schilbichthys garua.
garua, Schilbe	Cuv.	
gatensis, Leuciscus	Cuv.	Barilius gatensis.
gatensis, Opsarius	Bkr.	
Gaywah	N. W. P.	Labeo bicolor.
Geli pungti	Beng.	Barbus gelius.
gelius, Cyprinus	H. B.	Barbus gelius.
gelius, Systomus	Bkr.	
geto, Cobitis	H. B.	Botia dario.
Ghora chela	Assam.	Chela gora.
gibbosa, Cobitis	M'C.	Nemachilus turio.
gibbosus, Barbus	Cuv.	Barbus chrysopoma.
gibbosus, Systomus	M'C.	Barbus terio.
Gid	Punj.	Labeo ricnorhynchus.
Gid pakki	Can.	Barbus sarana.
Giddali	Punj.	Labeo bicolor.
Giddi kaoli	Hind.	Barbus sarana.
Gilland	Beng.	Barilius barila.
Goa chuppi	Ooriah.	Ambassis nama.
Goacherah	Beng.	Glyptosternum telchitta.
gobioides, Crossocheilos . .	Bkr.	Crossochilus mosario.
gobioides, Gonorhynchus .	M'C.	
Godhaee	Ooriah.	Corica soborna.
Godhaee	Ooriah.	Clupeoides soborna.
godiyava, Cyprinus	M'C.	Discognathus lamta.
gohama, Cirrhina	D.	Crossochilus gohama.
gohama, Cyprinus	H. B.	Crossochilus gohama.
goha, Barilius	Stein.	Bola goha.
goha, Cyprinus	H. B.	
goha, Opsarius	D.	Bola goha.

Name	Authority / Language	Species
Gollund	Ooriah.	Osteobrama rapax.
Gongituri	Ooriah.	Belone cancila.
gongota, Somileptes	Bkr.	Cobitis gongota.
gonius, Cyprinus	H. B.	Labeo gonius.
Gool gooli	Punj.	Oreinus sinuatus.
Goollah	Punj.	Bola goha.
Goolloo	Sind.	Gobius giuris.
Gooloowah	Punj.	Gobius giuris.
Goonch	Hind.	Bagarius yarellii.
Goongwah	Punj.	Callichrous bimaculatus.
Goongwahree	N. W. P.	
goongwaree, Hypophthalmus	S.	Pseudeutropius goongwaree.
Goontah	Beng.	Osteobrama alfrediana.
Goordah	Hind.	Osteobrama cotio.
Gootellah	Hind.	Cirrhina bata.
gora, Cyprinus	H. B.	Chela gora.
Gorayi	Beng.	Ophiocephalus punctatus.
Goreah	Assam.	Cirrhina dyochila.
Gorissa	Ooriah.	Ophiocephalus punctatus.
Gossiporah	Ooriah.	Nandus marmoratus.
gotyla, Garra	Stein.	Discognathus lamta.
gotyla, Gonorhynchus	Gray.	
gracilis, Barbus	J.	Barbus conirostris.
gracilis, Puntius	D.	
gracilis, Opsarius	M'C.	Bola goha.
gracilis, Ptyobranchus	M'C.	Moringua raitaborua.
Gra-e	Punj.	Ophiocephalus punctatus.
grandis, Botia	Gray.	Botia almorhæ.
grayi, Puntius	D.	Barbus melanampyx.
Gritti	Ooriah.	Rhynchobdella aculeata.
Gro-age	Punj.	Mastacemblus pancalus.
Grot	Cashmere.	Schizothorax hugelii.
guborni, Corica	Gray.	Clupeoides soborna.
Gudha	Punj.	Nandus marmoratus.
Gugah alli	Ooriah.	Macrones aor (young).
guganio, Cyprinus	H. B.	Barbus guganio.
Gulah	Ooriah.	Gobius giuris.
gularis, Tetrodon	H. B.	Tetrodon cutcutia.
gulio, Aspidobagrus	Bkr.	Macrones gulio.
gulio, Bagrus	Cuv.	
gulio, Pimelodus	H. B.	
gulioides, Bagrus	Bkr.	Macrones gulio.
Gunda	Ooriah.	Osteobrama alfrediana.
Gundum	Sind.	Notopterus chitala.
Guntea	Ooriah.	Macrones cavasius.
Gupkari	Ooriah.	Cobitis guntea.
Gurchee	Punj.	Mastacemblus pancalus.
Gurdun	Punj.	Nemachilus rupecola.
Gurha	Punj.	Schacra cirrhata.
Gurhi-e	Hind.	Ophiocephalus punctatus.
guthrianus, Ptyobranchus	M'C.	Moringua raitaborua.
guttata, Cobitis	M'C.	Nemachilus guttatus.
guttatus, Oreinus	M'C.	Oreinus sinuatus.
guttatus, Perilampus	M'C.	Chela laubuca.
Gutti	Ooriah.	Rhynchobdella aculeata.

malabaricus, Opsarius . .	J.	? Pteropsarion bakeri.
malabaricus, Perilampus .	J.	Danio osteographus (male).
malacopterus, Systomus . .	M'C.	Barbus cosuatis.
malacostomus, Gobio . . .	M'C.	Labeo falcatus.
Malgumaroo	R.	Anguilla bengalensis.
mangois, Pimelodus . . .	H. B.	Amblyceps mangois.
Manjil yete	Mal.	Macrones chryseus.
mannina, Clupanodon . .	H. B.	Chatoëssus mannina.
margarodes, Leuciscus . .	M'C.	Aspidoparia jaya?
marginatus, Ophiocephalus .	Cuv.	Ophiocephalus gachua.
Mar korava	Can.	Ophiocephalus gachua.
marmorata, Anguilla . . .	Kaup.	Anguilla bengalensis.
marmorata, Cobitis . . .	H.	Nemachilus marmoratus.
marmoratus, Mastacemblus	Cuv.	Mastacemblus armatus.
Mar pakkee	Can.	Barbus dorsalis.
Marpoo	R.	Clarias magur.
Marpu	Tel.	Saccobranchus fossilis.
marpus, Clarias	Cuv.	Clarias magur.
maya, Cobitis	S.	Cobitis gongota?
m'clellandi, Cyprinus . . .	Cuv.	Barbus immaculatus.
m'clellandi, Devario . . .	Bkr.	Danio devario.
m'clellandi, Gonorhynchus .	J.	Discognathus lamta.
megalepsis, Barbus . . .	M'C.	Barbus mosal.
megastomus, Opsarius . .	M'C.	Bola goha.
melanampyx, Labeo . . .	D.	Barbus melanampyx.
melanampyx, Puntius . . .	D.	
melanopterus, Panchax . .	Bkr.	Haplochilus panchax.
melas, Bagrus	Bkr.	Macrones gulio.
melettinus, Leuciscus . . .	Cuv.	Amblypharyngodon melettinus.
melettinus, Mola	D.	Amblypharyngodon melettinus.
menoda, Pimelodus . . .	H. B.	Macrones?
micracanthus, Capoeta . .	Günth.	Oreinus micracanthus.
microcephalus, Silurus . .	Cuv.	Callichrous chechra.
microcephalus, Wallago . .	Bkr.	
microlepidota, Rohita . . .	Günth.	Labeo cursa.
microlepis, Alausa	Cuv.	Clupea indica.
microlepis, Amblypharyngodon	Bkr.	Amblypharyngodon pellucidus.
microlepis, Leuciscus . . .	Bkr.	
microlepis, Rohtee . . .	D.	Osteobrama microlepis.
microlepis, Systomus . . .	Bly.	Osteobrama microlepis.
micronema, Danio	Bkr.	Danio osteographus.
micropogon, Batrachocephalus	Bkr.	Batrachocephalus mino.
micropogon, Cirrhina . . .	V.	Labeo calbasu.
Mileowah	Punj.	Rasbora daniconius.
militaris, Arius	Cuv.	Osteogeniosus militaris.
militaris, Silurus	Lin.	
minimus, Ophisurus . . .	M'C.	Ophichthys hyala.
mino, Ageniosus	H. B.	Batrachocephalus mino.
Mirgal	Hind.	Cirrhina mrigala.
Moah	Assam.	Amblypharyngodon mola.
modestus, Puntius	Kner.	Barbus modestus.
Moh	Punj.	Notopterus kapirat.
Mohaylee	N. W. P.	Labeo (tylognathus) bicolor.
Moinsia ballia	Ooriah.	Wallago attu.
Mola	N. W. P.	Nuria danrica.

mola, Cyprinus	H. B.	Amblypharyngodon mola.
monocera, Cobitis	M'C.	Nemachilus monoceros.
montana, Schistura . . .	M'C.	Nemachilus montanus.
montanus, Cobitis	J.	Nemachilus ?
montanus, Ophiocephalus .	M'C.	Ophiocephalus gachua.
mooreh, Cobitis	S.	Nemachilus moreh.
Mootaharee	Mal.	Nandus marmoratus.
Morah	Punj.	Labeo (tylognathus) ariza.
Morahkee	Sind.	Cirrhina mrigala.
morala, Cyprinus	H. B.	Labeo morala.
morar, Cyprinus	H. B.	Aspidoparia morar.
morar, Leuciscus	Bkr.	Aspidoparia morar.
morar, Leuciscus	M'C.	Aspidoparia morar.
morar, Morara	Bkr.	Aspidoparia morar ?
Morara	Ooriah.	Amblypharyngodon mola.
Mori	N. W. F.	Cirrhina mrigala.
Moriah	Punj.	Cachius atpar.
Morur	Hind.	Aspidoparia morar.
mosal, Cyprinus	H. B.	Barbus mosal.
mosal, Labeobarbus . . .	Stein.	Barbus chilinoides.
mosario, Cirrhina	D.	Crossochilus mosario.
mosario, Cyprinus	H. B.	Crossochilus mosario.
Mosoo	Tel.	Labeo cursa.
Mota	Tam.	Ophiocephalus punctatus.
motius, Clupanodon . . .	H. B.	Pellona motius.
motius, Clupea	Gray.	Pellona motius.
Motusi	Beng.	Pseudeutropius murius.
mrigala, Cyprinus	H. B.	Cirrhina mrigala.
Mucknee	Punj.	Ambassis nama.
Muckni	N. W. P.	Osteobrama cotio.
Muddibomiday	Tel.	Mastacemblus armatus.
Mugah	Beng.	Nemachilus mugah.
muhisa, Cyprinus	H. B.	Labeo morala ?
Mukka	Sind.	Chela phulo.
Mukkoor	Sind.	Ophiocephalus punctatus.
Mukni	Punj.	Amblypharyngodon mola.
Mullee	Punj.	Wallago attu.
Mulleer	Sind.	Macrones tengara.
mulleri, Silurus	Bkr.	Wallago attu.
mulleri, Wallago	Bkr.	Wallago attu.
Mullucheru	Mal.	Ambassis thomassi.
mullya, Chondrostoma . .	S.	Labeo mullya.
multidentata, Ptyobranchus	M'C.	Moringua raitaborua.
multiradiatus, Plotosus . .	Bkr.	Plotosus canius.
Mulwuj	Hind.	Nuria danrica.
Munduttee	Mal.	Barbus sarana.
Munglee ahnee	Sind.	Ailia bengalensis.
murius, Pimelodus	H. B.	Pseudeutropius murius.
Muri vacha	Hind.	Pseudeutropius murius.
Murrul	Hind.	Ophiocephalus striatus.
Mussayahri	Ooriah.	Rita kuturnee.
Mussooasah	Punj.	Nandus marmoratus.
mussullah, Barbus	S.	Barbus ?
Muti jella	Tel.	Macrones aor.
Muttah	R.	Ophiocephalus striatus.

mysorensis, Barbus . . .	J.	Barbus conirostris.
mysorensis, Cobitis . . .	J.	Nemachilus?
mysoricus, Silurus . . .	Cuv.	Callichrous canio.
mysoricus, Perilampus . .	J.	? Danio osteographus.
mystax, Clupea	Bloch.	Engraulis mystax.
Naharm	Ooriah.	Megalops cyprinoides.
Naharm	Hind.	Barbus mosal.
Nah-he	Punj.	Glyptosternum striatum.
Nah kellettee	Tamil.	Pseudeutropius sykesii.
Naim	N. W. P.	Cirrhina mrigala.
nalua, Chanda	H. B.	Ambassis nalua.
nama, Chanda	H. B.	Ambassis nama.
nancar, Cyprinus	H. B.	Labeo ? nancar.
Nandi buchua	Ooriah.	Eutropiichthys vacha.
nandina, Cyprinus	H. B.	Labeo nandina.
nandina, Rohita	Cuv.	Labeo nandina.
nandus, Coius	H. B.	Nandus marmoratus.
nangra, Pimelodus	H. B.	Macrones nangra.
Naolli	Ooriah.	Euctenogobius striatus (young).
nashii, Barbus	D.	Labeo nashii.
nasuta, Platycara	M'C.	Discognathus lamta.
nasutus, Discognathus . .	G.	Discognathus lamta.
nebulosa, Anguilla	M'C.	Anguilla bengalensis.
Neemuch	N. W. P.	Eutropiichthys vacha.
Nepura	Assam.	Labeo falcatus.
Netteli	Tamil.	Chela clupeoides.
neilgherriensis, Paradanio .	D.	Danio nilgherriensis.
nigroviridis, Tetrodon . . .	Procé.	Tetrodon fluviatilis.
Nilusu	Tel.	Barbus kolus.
Nooriee	Punj.	Saccobranchus fossilis.
notata, Platycara	Bly.	Discognathus lamta.
notopterus, Gymnosotus . .	Pal.	Notopterus kapirat.
novacula, Leuciscus . . .	V.	Chela novacula.
Now-u	Punj.	Glyptosternum striatum.
Nullagandu menu	Tel.	Labeo calbasu.
Nuna tengara	Beng.	Macrones gulio.
Nurhin	C. P.	Cirrhina mrigala.
oblonga, Cobitis	Cuv.	Acanthophthalmus pangia.
obtusus, Discognathus . . .	H.	Discognathus lamta.
ocellata, Cobitis	M'C.	Nemachilus botia.
ocellata, Rhynchobdella . .	Cuv.	Rhynchobdella aculeata.
ocellata, Schistura	M'C.	?
ocellatus, Macrognathus . .	H. B.	Rhynchobdella aculeata.
oculata, Cobitis	M'C.	Cobitis gongota.
oculatus, Bagrus	Cuv.	Macrones ?
ogilbii, Rohtee	S.	Osteobrama ogilbii.
oligolepis, Megalops . . .	Bkr.	Megalops cyprinoides.
Oolaree	Tamil.	Amblypharyngodon melettinus.
Ooloowey	Tamil.	Gobius giuris.
orientalis, Rhynchobdella .	Bloch.	Rhynchobdella aculeata.
ornatus, Notopterus	Gray.	Notopterus chitala.
osteographus, Perilampus .	M'C.	Danio osteographus.
Ovaree candee	Tamil.	Rasbora neilgherriensis.

Name	Authority	Species
owenii, Chela	S.	Chela phulo?
Paandra	Punj.	Barbus stigma.
Pabanoon	Sind.	Callichrous egertonii.
pabda, Silurus	H. B.	Callichrous pabda.
pabo, Schilbe	S.	Callichrous chechra.
pabo, Silurus	H. B.	Callichrous pabo.
Pahruah	Hind.	Aspidoparia jaya.
Pahtah	Punj.	Barilius cocsa.
palassii, Notopterus	Cuv.	Notopterus kapirat.
Pallu	Punj.	Callichrous bimaculatus.
pancalus, Macrognathus . .	H. B.	Mastacemblus pancalus.
panchax, Esox	H. B.	Haplochilus panchax.
panchax, Panchax	Cant.	Haplochilus panchax.
Pandi pakkee	Can.	Discognathus lamta.
pangasius, Pimelodus . . .	H. B.	Pangasius buchanani.
Pangchak	Beng.	Haplochilus panchax.
pangia, Cobitis	H. B.	Acanthophthalmus pangia.
pangusia, Cyprinus	H. B.	Labeo pangusia.
pangut, Rohtee	S.	Barbus cosuatis.
Paochar	Punj.	Aspidoparia morar.
Paraga	Can.	Amblypharyngodon melettinus.
Para korava	Tamil.	Ophiocephalus gachua.
Parparal	Tel.	Mastacemblus pancalus.
Parrah perlee	Mal	Barbus parrah.
Parri	N. W. F.	Notopterus kapirat.
parvidentata, Ptyobranchus .	M'C.	Moringua raitaborua.
Patia kerundi	Ooriah.	Barbus stigma.
Patoca	Beng.	Tetrodon.
Paungsi	Hind.	Labeo morala.
Paunia puice	Ooriah.	Pellona dussumieri.
Pauni eyri	Tamil.	Anabas scandens.
pausio, Cyprinus	H. B.	Labeo?
pausius, Cyprinus	H. B.	Labeo morala.
pavimentatus, Arius	Cuv.	Rita pavimentata.
pavonacea, Cobitis	M'C.	Nemachilus pavonaceus.
Peedah	Sind.	Ambassis lala.
pellucidus, Leuciscus . . .	M'C.	Amblypharyngodon pellucidus.
Pencha	Beng.	Engraulis telara.
pentophthalmus, Mastacemblus	Gron.	Rhynchobdella aculeata.
perlee, Puntius	D.	Barbus chola.
peronii, Pimelodus	Cuv.	Hemipimelodus peronii.
Perowa	Hind.	Rasbora daniconius.
Persee	Hind.	Barilius barila.
perseus, Perilampus	M'C.	Chela perseus.
petrophilus, Gonorhynchus .	M'C.	Oreinus richardsonii?
Pettohee	Sind.	Barbus titius.
phacra, Cyprinus	H. B.	Schacra cirrhata.
phaiosoma, Gobius	Bkr.	Gobius giuris.
Pharbadun	Sind.	Chela bacaila.
Pharrie	Sind.	Chela gora.
Phasa	Beng.	Engraulis telara.
phasa, Engraulis	Cuv.	Engraulis telara.
„ Clupea	H. B.	Engraulis telara.
Phoksha	Hind.	Tetrodon cutcutia.

Name	Authority	Synonym
pholicephalus, Opsarius	M'C.	Chela gora.
Pholoe	Beng.	Notopterus kapirat.
Phool dhok	Hind.	Ophiocephalus punctatus.
Phool murrul	Hind.	Ophiocephalus marulius.
Phool verarl	Tam.	
phoxochila, Cobitis	M'C.	Nemachilus phoxochilus.
phula, Chanda	H. B.	Ambassis nama.
Phul chela	Beng.	Chela phulo.
phulo, Cyprinus	H. B.	
Phutoni pungti	Beng.	Barbus phutonio.
phutonio, Cyprinus	H. B.	Barbus phutonio.
phutonio, Systomus	Bkr.	
Pichru	Sind.	Trichogaster fasciatus.
Pila kuturnee	Hind.	Macrones chryseus.
pinnauratus, Cyclocheilichthys	D.	Barbus pinnauratus.
pinnauratus, Puntius	D.	
piscatorius, Barilius	D.	Barilius alburnus.
piscatorius, Opsarius	M'C.	Barilius alburnus.
Pitha kerundi	Ooriah.	Barbus chola.
Pitul kas	Hind.	Etroplus suratensis.
plagiostomus, Schizothorax	H.	? Oreinus plagiostomus.
planiceps, Ophiocephalus	Cuv.	Ophiocephalus striatus.
plumbea, Cirrhina	Cuv.	Cirrhina ?
Poaree candee	Tamil.	Barbus carnaticus.
Pobta	Ooriah.	Callichrous checlira.
Pobta	Punj.	Callichrous bimaculatus.
Pohpree	Sind.	Barbus sarana.
Poikee	Sind.	Wallago attu.
polyacantha, Rhynchobdella	Bloch.	Mastacemblus armatus.
Pompiah	N. W. P.	Ambassis nama.
Poncha geraldi	Ooriah.	Barilius rerio.
ponticeriana, Colisa	Cuv.	Trichogaster fasciatus.
ponticerianus, Mastacemblus	Cuv.	Mastacemblus armatus.
Ponundi	Tel.	Trichogaster fasciatus.
Poola chapa	Tel.	Ophiocephalus marulius.
Poomeen candee	Tamil.	Barbus mosal.
Poonattee	Tamil.	Silondia gangetica.
porcellus, Tylognathus	H.	Labeo porcellus.
Potah	Hind.	Barbus sarana.
potail, Cyprinus	S.	? Labeo.
potamophilus, Tetrodon	Bkr.	Tetrodon fluviatilis.
Pottiah	Hind.	Barbus stigma.
presbyter, Leuciscus	Cuv.	Barbus presbyter.
progeneius, Barbus	M'C.	Barbus mosal.
Psetta kelettee	Tamil.	Macrones punctatus.
psilopterimus, Perilampus	M'C.	Cachius atpar.
Puckwahree	Punj.	Barilius cocsa.
Puddoo	Sind.	Ambassis nama.
Pud du ah	Punj.	Callomystax gagata (young).
Pufta	Hind.	Callichrous bimaculatus.
Pulli	Ooriah.	Notopterus kapirat.
Pullooree	Punj.	Clupea indica.
Pul lut tay	Mal.	Etroplus maculatus.
Pultosi	Beng.	Schilbichthys garua.
Pulwuah	Punj.	Callichrous egertonii.

Name	Authority	Species
Talla maya	Tel.	Amblypharyngodon mola.
Tambra	Bombay.	Catla buchanani ?
Tampara	Ooriah.	Engraulis telara.
teekanee, Chela	S.	Chela (?)
Teepah benki	Ooriah.	Tetrodon cutcutia.
telara, Clupea	H. B.	Engraulis telara.
telaroides, Engraulis	Bkr.	Engraulis taty.
telchitta, Pimelodus	H. B.	Glyptosternum telchitta.
Tellarree	Punj.	Crossochilus gohama.
tengana, Bagrus	Cuv.	Macrones tengana.
tengana, Pimelodus	H. B.	
tengara, Bagrus	Cuv.	Macrones tengara.
tengara, Pimelodus	H. B.	
Tengara	Punj.	Macrones { tengara. lamarri.
tenuifilis, Engraulis	Cuv.	Engraulis taty.
terio, Cyprinus	H. B.	Barbus terio.
Teri pungti	Beng.	Barbus terio.
testudineus, Anthias	Bloch.	Anabas scandens.
testudineus, Amphiprion	Bloch.	
testudineus, Sparus	Shaw.	
testudineus, Anabas	Cuv.	
testudo, Lutjanus	Lacép.	
tetrarupagus, Systomus	M'C.	Barbus tetrarupagus.
Tharlee	Tamil.	Saccobranchus fossilis.
thermalis, Cobitis	Cuv.	Lepidocephalichthys thermalis.
thermalis, Leuciscus	Cuv.	Barbus thermalis.
thermoicos, Esomus	Kner.	Nuria danrica.
thermoicos, Nuria	Cuv.	
thermophilos, Nuria	Cuv.	
thermophilus Perilampus	M'C.	
ticto, Cyprinus	H. B.	Barbus ticto.
ticto, Rohtee	S.	? Barbus ticto.
tila, Cyprinus	H. B.	Barilius cocsa.
tileo, Cyprinus	H. B.	Barilius tileo.
Tilleah	Punj.	Glyptosternum telchitta.
tincoides, Rohita	Cuv.	Labeo cursa.
titius, Barbus	G.	Barbus tetrarupagus.
titius, Cyprinus	H. B.	Barbus titius.
Tit pungti	Beng.	
Took	Punj.	Chela punjabensis.
Toolee	Mal.	Labeo dussumieri.
tor, Cyprinus	H. B.	Barbus mosal.
trachacanthus, Bagrus	Cuv.	Macrones ?
trachipomus, Bagrus	Cuv.	Arius gagorides.
trifoliatus, Anabas	Kaup.	Anabas scandens.
trilineatus, Glyptothorax	Bly.	Glyptosternum trilineatum.
tripunctatus, Systomus	J.	Barbus ticto.
tristis, Systomus	J.	Barbus ?
Tsikidundu	Tel.	Gobius giuris.
Turi	Ooriah.	Mastacemblus pancalus.
turio, Cobitis	H. B.	Nemachilus turio.
typus, Gagata	Bkr.	Callomystax gagata.
Undala	Hind.	Mugil corsula.

LIST OF REFERENCES AND ABBREVIATIONS.

R.—P. Russell. (Fishes of Vizagapatam, 1803.)
H. B.—Dr. Hamilton, formerly Buchanan. (Fishes of the Ganges, 1822), etc.
H.—J. Heckel. (Fische aus Cashmere, Wien, 1838.)
Gray.—J. E. Gray. (Illustrations of Indian Zoology, 1830–32.)
M'C.—Dr. J. M'Clelland. (Indian Cyprinidæ, 1839; and other papers published in the Journals of the Asiatic Society of Bengal.)
S.—Col. Sykes. (Fishes of the Dukhun, 1841; and other papers in the Transactions of the Zoological Society of London.)
J.—Dr. Jerdon. (Fresh-water Fishes of Southern India, 1849; in Madras Journal of Literature and Science, and other publications.)
Bly.—Edward Blyth. (Papers in the Journals of the Asiatic Society, Bengal, 1858–60.)
Bkr.—Dr. P. Von Blecker. (Atlas Ichthyologique Amsterdam, 1862–72; and many other publications.)
D.—Dr. Day. (Indian Cyprinidæ, and other papers in the Journals of the Asiatic Society, Bengal, and also of the Zoological Society.)
G.—Dr. A. Günther. (Catalogue of the Fishes in the British Museum. 8 vols. 1859–1870, etc.)
Cuv.—Baron Cuvier, and Valenciennes. (Histoire Naturelle de Poissons. 22 vols. Paris, 1828–49; and other works.)
V.—Mon. A. Vallenciennes.
Pl.—Lieut.-Col. R. L. Playfair.
Bloch.—M. E. Bloch. (Systema Ichthyologiæ; revised by J. G. Schneider.)
L.—Linnæus.
Lacèp.—Comte de Lacepède.
Stein.—F. Steindachner.
Kner.—R. Kner.
Pal.—P. S. Pallas.
Gro.—L. T. Gronow.
Shaw.—George Shaw.
Kaup.—J. J. Kaup.
Ow.—Owen.
Procé.
Peters.
Dald.—Capt. Daldorf. (Linnæan Transactions.)
Rich.—Sir John Richardson.
M.—Muller and Troschel.
Cant.—Dr. Cantor.
Bon.—Bonnaterre.

PROVINCES.

Hind.—Hindostan generally.
Beng.—Bengal.
N. W. P.—North West Provinces.
Punj.—Punjab.
N. W. F.—North West frontier.
Assam.—North East frontier.
Cash.—Cashmere.
Mal.—Malabar.
C. P.—Central Provinces.
Can.—Canara.
Deccan.
Sind.
Nepal.
Oudh.
Bhutan.
Bombay.

DIALECTS.

Tamil.
Tel.—Telegoo.
Ooriah.
Mah.—Mahratta.